Women's Rights, Feminism, and Politics in the United States

Mary Lyndon Shanley
Vassar College

with an

Introduction and Epilogue

by

Shelby Lewis

1988

American Political Science Association
1527 New Hampshire Avenue, N.W.
Washington, D.C. 20036

The development of Women's Rights, Feminism, and Politics in the United States was supported by a grant from the Fund for the Improvement of Post-Secondary Education. That grant also supported the review and field testing of the monograph. This is a revised edition that incorporates the recommendations of faculty and students who read the original test edition (1983). The publication of the revised edition has been approved by the Association's Committee on Education. The views expressed in the book are those of Mary Lyndon Shanley and Shelby Lewis and not of the American Political Science Association.

ISBN-0-915654-79-2

CONTENTS

Series Preface

When it comes to questions of "power," especially in "public affairs," women somehow still tend to get dropped from consideration as viable "political" beings. It is thus more often the case than not that we approach the study and teaching of United States government and politics from male-centered perspectives. Why is this so? What would the study and teaching of United States government and politics look like from women's diverse perspectives? What would the field of American Government and Politics, much less the discipline of political science look like, if the hierarchies associated with gender, race, and economic class in the discipline and in its subject matter were transformed? These are some of the questions that the various units of CITIZENSHIP AND CHANGE: WOMEN AND AMERICAN POLITICS *begin* to address.

I stress "begin" because, in the experiences of many who have been involved in such endeavors, the process of transforming gender, race, and class hierarchies in bodies of knowledge is neither easy nor quickly accomplished. The process is not easy because in order to transform a structure we must also grasp the complexities of its construction. The process is not quick because transforming structured bodies of knowledge involves changing political consciousness as well. Such transformations may meet resistances along the way and thus do not happen overnight. Having only begun, we still have much challenging theoretical and practical work to do. But, at least, we have begun.

The "we" in this particular endeavor is an institutional complex of organizations, committees, faculty and students. The American Political Science Association, through its Director of Educational Affairs, its Committee on the Status of Women in the Profession and its Committee on Education, received a three-year grant (1981-1983) from the U. S. Department of Education Fund for the Improvement of Post-Secondary Education for a project to integrate the scholarship on women and politics into introductory courses in American Government and Politics. The project called for setting up a Task Force on Women and American Government to define the theoretical parameters of the undertaking, to write the texts that would serve as the vehicles for integrating feminist scholarship into courses, and to introduce the texts to political scientists in workshops at national and regional professional meetings. The texts then were field-tested by interested faculty and students across the country in a variety of college campus settings. Each text was also evaluated by scholars in the field. Texts were revised in response to field-test evaluations and peer reviews before final publication by the APSA. The text you now hold in your hands, therefore, owes its existence not only to its author or authors but also to the larger institutional context in which they worked.

Many thanks are due to all the organizations and persons involved in seeing the project through to its conclusion. These include the Committee on the Status of Women, chaired at the initiation of the project by Susan Woodward and during the implementation phase by Susette Talarico; the Committee on Education, chaired at the initiation stage by Judith A. Gillespie and during implementation by Carey McWilliams; and above all the Director of Educational Affairs, from initiation to conclusion of the project, Sheilah Mann, and her assistant, Judy Caruthers. For financial and organizational support thanks go to FIPSE and the APSA. Thanks also go to members of the Task Force, whose collective discussions, in addition to their various writings, enabled the project to encompass the breadth that our beginnings did manage to reach: Beverly Cook, Irene Diamond, Joyce Gelb, Leslie Goldstein, Anne Harper, Cynthia Harrison, Milda Hedblom, Ethel Klein, Shelby Lewis, Karen O'Connor, Diane Pinderhughes, Virginia Sapiro, Mary Shanley, Sarah Slavin, Judith Stiehm, Susette Talarico, and especially to our late colleague, Clement Vose, to whom we dedicate these units. Last, but not least, thanks go to the many faculty and students who field-tested the units.

Speaking for "we," I hope that you find as much inspiration and excitement as we have in the process of integrating feminist scholarship with your studies and teachings of United States politics. We hope that you find challenging rather than off-putting the difficulties of transforming political science.

Diane L. Fowlkes
Chair, Task Force on Women and American
Government
Atlanta, Georgia, 1987

Author's Preface

This unit is intended to introduce the reader to the relationship between feminism and American politics. It contains a history of women's political activities and of feminist ideology in the United States, along with a series of documents which are central primary sources for reconstructing those histories. These provide students with manifestoes, trial proceedings, newspaper articles, Supreme Court decisions, and other materials which both reflected and shaped the status of women in the United States.

Understanding women's relationship to the American polity requires a three-fold investigation: What was the civil and political status of women at various points in our history? What did feminists *say* about that status? What did feminists *do* to improve women's status? This unit will discuss each of these topics, but will give primary emphasis to the tradition of feminist protest and analysis of American politics.

This enterprise challenges many of the common assumptions made about American political ideology and history. We tend to regard the Declaration of Independence and the Preamble to the Constitution as the heart of our political credo, establishing the principle that "all men are created equal and are endowed . . . with certain inalienable rights." What are we to make of the assertion of the signers of the "Declaration of Sentiments" at Seneca Falls that the American Revolution and subsequent political reforms had in fact given political freedom to half

the adult polity, to men and not to women? We have usually studied movements for black liberation and women's liberation as quite distinct struggles, ignoring (and thereby banishing from our national self-understanding) ideas and activities of those black women who insisted upon the reality of both racial and sexual oppression in the American polity. How are we to understand Ida B. Wells' and others' analyses of the ways in which sexual and racial fears are used to reinforce one another? Many people think of "feminism" and the "feminist movement" as recent phenomena, a legacy of the turbulent reforming spirit of the 1960s. How will it shape our understanding of contemporary feminism to realize that its roots extend back to the earliest days of our political history, and that feminism today draws upon a long and continuous political tradition? This assessment of American feminism in relationship to American politics will, I hope, help teachers and students alike to realize the ways in which the omission of such materials from our political histories and analyses contributes to the perpetuation of women's political disabilities as well as to the distortion of our common heritage.

I would like to thank Cynthia Harrison for her reviews and constructive comments. Members of the Task Force for the project, "Citizenship and Change: Women and American Politics," also commented helpfully on this unit.

These chapters are dedicated to Jean Reeder Smith and Ann Congleton, superb teachers.

Chapter 1

The Beginning of an Organized Women's Movement: Abolitionism and Suffrage

To understand the emergence of feminism as a *political movement*, one must look both at its intellectual roots and at the links between feminism and other political movements of nineteenth century America. Feminism, an ideology which insists upon women's value and promotes equality between the sexes, was closely linked with Enlightenment ideas of the natural rights of all individuals; with utopian ideas of new forms of community which gave rise to experiments like Robert Owen's New Harmony in Indiana, Brooke Farm in Massachusetts, and Frances Wright's Nashoba in Tennessee; and with religious evangelicalism and notions of the worth of every soul before God. The rhetoric of the American Revolution drew upon and disseminated the idea that "all men are created equal" and are endowed with certain "inalienable rights." Women such as Abigail Adams and Mercy Otis Warren saw that women's political and legal rights did not yet come up to these ideals, and Adams admonished her husband to "remember the ladies" when creating the new republic. In *A Vindication of the Rights of Women* (1790), Mary Wollstonecraft, an Englishwoman, argued that the "rights of man" should refer to the rights of all "humankind," not just to males. The idea that society was formed by a social contract, entered into by individuals who were "free and equal" in the state of nature was central to many political thinkers Americans revered, such as John Locke, Jean-Jacques Rousseau, and Thomas Jefferson. The logic of Wollstonecraft's argument that women shared in that initial equality and hence could not be excluded from equal participation in civil society had a strong hold on many feminists and linked them with parts of this country's most deeply cherished principles.

The ideas of utopian socialists such as Charles Fourier, Saint-Simon, Robert Owen, and Frances Wright, and those of the New England Transcendentalists were also important to American feminists. Needless to say, these people varied widely in their theories of human psychology and social evolution. They were important to feminism not for any single idea, but because of their belief in the malleability of human social relationships and institutions. Frances (Fanny) Wright's (1795–1852) experimental community, Nashoba, which existed from 1825 to 1829, for example, abjured legally enforced marriage, advocated racial intermarriage, and abandoned traditional Christian teaching for a moral system based on Benthamite utilitar-

ianism. Nashoba ultimately succumbed to disease and financial problems, but its failure was perhaps not as important as the example it gave to those who desired transformations in personal relationships as well as in institutional structures. While Liberal political theory gave women the concepts of "equal rights," utopian thought and communities held forth the hope of genuine respect and reciprocity between men and women, and nourished these broader dreams of the feminists.

Religious revivalism and the Protestant tradition also fed American feminism. It is true that much Judeo-Christian teaching defended social hierarchy and the dominance of male over female, but the rise of evangelicalism in the early nineteenth century was rooted in Puritan traditions of the equality of all souls before God, of personal revelation, and of witness to God's word by every individual. The Second Great Awakening (1794–1835) spurred American evangelicals to the belief that salvation depended upon morally responsible action to eradicate social evil and injustice. During this period many women poured their energies into moral reform societies, missionary societies, educational efforts, and anti-slavery work. Many of them eventually also worked on behalf of women's rights.

The traditional date for the beginning of the women's rights movement in the United States is July 19, 1848. On that day some three hundred women and men gathered in a Methodist church in Seneca Falls, New York, to protest the legal, economic, and social subordination of women. The meeting was convened by Elizabeth Cady Stanton (1815–1902) and Lucretia Mott (1793–1880). Stanton and Mott had met and became friends eight years earlier while attending the World Anti-Slavery Convention of 1840 in London. Lucretia Mott and her husband James were Philadelphia Quakers, prominent figures in the abolitionist movement, and delegates to the Convention. Elizabeth Cady Stanton had married Henry Stanton, also a delegate, and their trip doubled as a honeymoon. A dispute broke out at the Convention over the issue of whether women delegates could be seated as voting members. Many from the United States had expected nothing less, but after heated debate women were granted only observer status. Henry Stanton spoke on the women's behalf, as did William Lloyd Garrison. Garrison and Charles Redmond, a Black abolitionist from Maine, refused to take their seats as delegates in protest against women's exclusion. Discussion of slavery and of this dismissal of women brought Elizabeth Cady Stanton and Lucretia Mott together. In her autobiography Stanton describes the importance of the World Anti-Slavery Convention to her political education:

> These were the first women I had ever met who believed in the equality of the sexes and who did not believe in the popular orthodox religion. The acquaintance of Lucretia Mott, who was a broad, liberal thinker on politics, religion, and all questions of reform, opened to me a new world of thought. As we walked about to see the sights of London, I embraced every opportunity to talk with her. It was intensely gratifying to hear all that, through years of doubt, I had dimly thought, so freely discussed by other women. . . . (Stanton, 1971, 83)

Stanton and Mott vowed to hold a conference to air their views on women's disabilities upon their return to the United States. Although that meeting was very much delayed, in 1848 they revived their plans for a women's rights convention. They posted handbills in the region around Stanton's home in upstate New York, and invited prominent abolitionists to attend. Frederick Douglass, who was an ex-slave and abolitionist, came from Rochester, and publicized subsequent women's rights activities in his paper *The North Star*; Horace Greely's *Tribune* did the same. Indeed, early feminists relied extensively on anti-slavery organizations for membership, experienced speakers, and newspaper publicity and editorial support. Without the already-existing infrastructure of the anti-slavery movement, the tiny women's rights movement would have had little impact.

Despite the feminists' links to abolitionism, however, no black women attended the Seneca Falls convention. Some black women had, however, been deeply involved in the issues of abolition and women's rights. Maria Stewart of Boston, who published essays in Garrison's *Liberator*, delivered several lectures on black women's plight and their aspirations in 1832 and 1834. She encountered such hostility as a woman speaking in public, however, that she moved to New York City, where she worked for the North Star Association and attended the Anti-Slavery Convention of American Women, but abjured the public platform. In 1837 Angelina and Sarah Grimke had criticized the New York Female Anti-Slavery Society for not involving black women in their work, and segregation in women's rights and abolitionist organizations continued to be the norm, even as both black and white women worked strenuously in these causes. (Sterling, 1984, 153–159; Davis, 1981, 58)

The "Declaration of Sentiments" and "Resolutions" adopted at Seneca Falls, and a speech given by Sojourner Truth at a women's rights convention in Akron, Ohio, in 1851 reflect many of the aspects of this phase of American feminism. [See Documents 1 and 2.] The "Declaration of Sentiments" began with language taken directly from the Declaration of Independence of 1776, a borrowing which linked the women's protest to the liberal tradition of natural rights and government by consent. It focused on two legal issues which underlay women's right to "throw off such government": women's lack of the vote, and the common law doctrine of spousal unity which took away a woman's separate legal status when she married. As a result a wife could not sign contracts, sue or be sued, or even make a will without her husband's consent; her earnings were legally his, and he had right to the custody of their minor children. The critique of these legal rules also drew heavily on liberal notions that no person could justly be deprived of rights or liberties without explicit consent or except as punishment for a crime.

The preamble of the Seneca Falls "Declaration" referred to unjust "government," but the list of abuses included not only laws but "repeated injuries and usurpations on the part of man toward woman, having in direct object the establishment of an absolute tyranny over her." Occupations such as the ministry, law, and medicine were closed to women, as were institutions of higher education. Here the middle-class character of the women of Seneca Falls was clearly evident—they did not protest factory conditions or sweated labor. Nor, despite their strong interest in abolitionism, did they protest here the absolute subjection of slave women. They similarly ignored the violent removal of Native American women from the lands appropriated by European settlers.

Finally, the Seneca Falls convention denounced the sexual domination of women by men, particularly the sexual double-standard. In many jurisdictions, a single act of adultery by a wife was cause for divorce, but a man could not be divorced even for repeated adultery unless it was combined with physical cruelty, bigamy or incest. The denunciation of attitudes which tolerated "moral delinquencies" in men but not in women was not, however, intended to imply that women should be as free as men. Rather, men should henceforth be held to the rigorous moral code which ruled their wives and sisters.

As the participants had urged, other women's rights conventions were held; between 1850–1860 there were national conventions every year except 1857. (Flexner, 1959, 81) These meetings were often called by those working in anti-slavery organizations who suffered not only the wrongs of women's legal disabilities but also the frustration of being unable to work effectively for black people as long as there existed such strong prejudice against women speaking in public.

In 1851 the women's rights convention in Akron nearly foundered because, as the presiding officer Frances Gage reported:

> There were very few women in those days who dared to 'speak in meeting'; and the august teachers of the people [traditional clergymen] were seemingly getting the better of us, while the boys in the galleries and the sneerers in the pews, were hugely enjoying the discomfiture, as they supposed, of the 'strong-minded.'

At this point Sojourner Truth, an ex-slave active in abolitionist work, rose to speak. [See Document 2.] Both her commanding physical presence and her account of her life in slavery refuted the argument that women were too "weak" or delicate to engage in business, politics, or the professions. Her speech effectively linked women's rights and Black rights, charging white males to relinquish even a bit of their power and authority to those without their privileges. Most importantly, her speech implicitly rejected the usual rhetoric which talked about "women's rights" on the one hand and "Negro rights" on the other, as if all Blacks were male. Phyllis Marynick Palmer has pointed out that Gage characterized Sojourner truth as "fierce and yet maternal, a leader and yet a servant and 'mammy,'" who had "'taken us up in her strong arms and carried us safely over the slough of difficulty. . . .'" The image of white women being cradled in a black woman's arms, remarked Palmer, had a lasting appeal as a challenge to the stereotypes of female incapacity. It is also significant that Gage did not portray Truth as much as a co-worker or sister, as a mother or savior. (Palmer, 1983, 153)

During the 1850s the small group interested in women's rights grew slowly. It was during this period that Susan B. Anthony (1820–1906) began to work for women's rights. Anthony was born into an anti-slavery Quaker family, and became a schoolteacher and then a temperance worker. In 1851 Amelia Bloomer, who published the feminist newspaper *The Lily*, introduced Susan Anthony to Elizabeth Cady Stanton; the two became life-long friends and political allies. In 1852 they founded the New York State Women's Temperance Society, wholly under women's control. Their platform included not only temperance, but the much more radical measures of women suffrage ("so that women may vote on this great political and social evil") and liberalized divorce laws allowing women to divorce husbands who were drunkards. (DuBois, 1981, 17) These latter measures proved to be too much for most of the membership, and at the next annual meeting the demand for suffrage and liberalized divorce law were repudiated. Stanton was voted out of the presidency, and Anthony withdrew from the vice-presidency. But their political alliance was cemented, wedding Stanton's more radical and broad-based feminism to Anthony's unsurpassed organizational skill.

They next turned their efforts to obtaining a married women's property law in New York state through petitions to and testimony before the state legislature. In 1860 the legislature finally enacted full property, parental and widows' rights for New York women. During this time Stanton and Anthony also kept up their ties with the anti-slavery movement. They were in constant touch with others who shared their dedication to abolishing slavery and procuring women's rights as well; Lucretia Mott, Lucy Stone, Ernestine Rose, and Pauline Wright Davis were all good friends and political comrades. In 1857 Anthony took Lucy Stone's place as a paid organizer for the American Anti-Slavery Society, which agitated against slavery outside of electoral politics, and in 1860 Stanton addressed the AASS on the link between women's rights and freedom for the slaves. The outbreak of the Civil War in 1861 galvanized the attention of the entire nation on issues of war and of slavery, and suspended women's rights agitation until hostilities ceased.

Even such a brief survey of the origins of organized feminism highlights several features of the early movement which are important to both an historical and a theoretical understanding of American feminism. First: it is deeply rooted in several strains of American social and political thought, including utopian thought and experimental communities, evangelical religion and moral reform, and liberal individualism and natural rights ideology. Second, it has from the beginning demanded a reformation of male/female relations. A common misunderstanding of feminism is that it changed in the 1960s from a movement for women's political rights alone to one concerned with marriage, sexual relations, and matters of personal "liberation." On the contrary, most early nineteenth century feminists were more concerned with the domestic subjection of women and the sexual double standard than they were with obtaining the vote. Third, the Seneca Falls "Declaration of Sentiments" forthrightly asserted its authors' belief that sex constituted what we would call a "class," men having a vested interest in maintaining their dominance. The borrowing of the language of the Declaration of Independence showed, in addition, the authors' conviction that the Revolution of 1776 was incomplete, that it had not, in fact, freed any women from political disability. Fourth, the feminists of

the mid-nineteenth century were by-and-large political radicals (abolitionism was unacceptable even to many Republicans), and the majority of them were white and middle-class. Throughout the century these women exhibited political iconoclasm and risk-taking combined with class and racial bias. Subsequent chapters will explore the continuing influence of these characteristics on the development of American feminism.

DOCUMENT 1

'Declaration of Sentiments' and 'Resolutions' adopted by the Seneca Falls Convention of 1848

When, in the course of human events, it becomes necessary for one portion of the family of man to assume among the people of the earth a position different from that which they have hitherto occupied, but one to which the laws of nature and of nature's God entitle them, a decent respect to the opinions of mankind requires that they should declare the causes that impel them to such a course.

We hold these truths to be self-evident: that all men and women are created equal; that they are endowed by their Creator with certain inalienable rights; that among these are life, liberty, and the pursuit of happiness; that to secure these rights governments are instituted, deriving their just powers from the consent of the governed. Whenever any form of government becomes destructive of these ends, it is the right of those who suffer from it to refuse allegiance to it, and to insist upon the institution of a new government, laying its foundation on such principles, and organizing its powers in such form, as to them shall seem most likely to effect their safety and happiness. Prudence indeed, will dictate that governments long established should not be changed for light and transient causes; and accordingly all experience hath shown that mankind are more disposed to suffer, while evils are sufferable, than to right themselves by abolishing the forms to which they were accustomed. But when a long train of abuses and usurpations, pursuing invariably the same object evinces a design to reduce them under absolute despotism, it is their duty to throw off such government, and to provide new guards for their future security. Such has been the patient sufferance of the women under this government, and such is now the necessity which constrains them to demand the equal station to which they are entitled.

The history of mankind is a history of repeated injuries and usurpations on the part of man toward woman, having in direct object the establishment of an absolute tyranny over her. To prove this, let facts be submitted to a candid world.

He has never permitted her to exercise her inalienable right to the elective franchise.

He has compelled her to submit to laws, in the formation of which she had no voice.

He has withheld from her rights which are given to the most ignorant and degraded men—both natives and foreigners.

Source: Stanton, Elizabeth, Susan B. Anthony and Matilda J. Gage, eds., *History of Women Suffrage*, I, Rochester, N.Y.: Fowler and Wells, 1881–1922. Reprinted in O'Neill, William L., *The Woman Movement* (London: Allen and Unwin, 1969), 108–111.

Having deprived her of this first right of a citizen, the elective franchise, thereby leaving her without representation in the halls of legislation, he has oppressed her on all sides.

He has made her, if married, in the eye of the law, civilly dead.

He has taken from her all right in property, even to the wages she earns.

He has made her, morally, an irresponsible being, as she can commit many crimes with impunity, provided they be done in the presence of her husband. In the covenant of marriage, she is compelled to promise obedience to her husband, he becoming, to all intents and purposes, her master—the law giving him power to deprive her of her liberty, and to administer chastisement.

He has so framed the laws of divorce, as to what shall be the proper causes, and in case of separation, to whom the guardianship of the children shall be given, as to be wholly regardless of the happiness of women—the law, in all cases, going upon a false supposition of the supremacy of man, and giving all power into his hands.

After depriving her of all rights as a married woman, if single, and the owner of property, he has taxed her to support a government which recognizes her only when her property can be made profitable to it.

He has monopolized nearly all the profitable employments, and from those she is permitted to follow, she receives but a scanty remuneration. He closes against her all the avenues to wealth and distinction which he considers most honorable to himself. As a teacher of theology, medicine, or law, she is not known.

He has denied her the facilities for obtaining a thorough education, all colleges being closed against her.

He allows her in Church, as well as State, but a subordinate position, claiming Apostolic authority for her exclusion from the ministry, and, with some exceptions, from any public participation in the affairs of the Church.

He has created a false public sentiment by giving to the world a different code of morals for men and women, by which moral delinquencies which exclude women from society, are not only tolerated, but deemed of little account in man.

He has usurped the prerogative of Jehovah himself, claiming it as his right to assign for her a sphere of action, when that belongs to her conscience and to her God.

He has endeavored, in every way that he could, to destroy her confidence in her own powers, to lessen her self-respect, and to make her willing to lead a dependent and abject life.

Now in view of this entire disfranchisement of one-half the people of this country, their social and religious degradation—in view of the unjust laws above mentioned, and because women do feel themselves aggrieved, oppressed, and fraudulently deprived of their most sacred rights, we insist that they have immediate admission to all the rights and privileges which belong to them as citizens of the United States.

In entering upon the great work before us, we anticipate no small amount of misconception, misrepresentation, and ridicule; but we shall use every instrumentality within our power to effect our object. We shall employ agents, circulate tracts, petition the State and National legislatures, and endeavor to enlist the pulpit and the press in our behalf. We hope this Convention will be followed by a series of Conventions embracing every part of the country.

The following resolutions were discussed by Lucretia Mott, Thomas and Mary Ann McClintock, Amy Post, Catharine A. F. Stebbins, and others, and were adopted:

WHEREAS, The great precept of nature is conceded to be, that "man shall pursue his own true and substantial happiness." Blackstone in his Commentaries remarks, that this law of Nature being coeval with mankind, and dictated by God himself, is of course superior in obligation to any other. It is binding over all the globe, in all countries and at all times; no human laws are of any validity if contrary to this, and such of them as are valid, derive all their force, and all their validity, and all their authority, mediately and immediately, from this original; therefore;

Resolved, that such laws as conflict, in any way, with the true and substantial happiness of woman, are contrary to the great precept of nature and of no validity, for this is "superior in obligation to any other."

Resolved, That all laws which prevent woman from occupying such a station in society as her conscience shall dictate, or which place her in a position inferior to that of man, are contrary to the great precept of nature, and therefore of no force or authority.

Resolved, That woman is man's equal—was intended to be so by the Creator, and the highest good of the race demands that she should be recognized as such.

Resolved, that the women of this country ought to be enlightened in regard to the laws under which they live, that they may no longer publish their degradation by declaring themselves satisfied with their present position, nor their ignorance, by asserting that they have all the rights they want.

Resolved, That inasmuch as man, while claiming for himself intellectual superiority, does accord to woman moral superiority, it is pre-eminently his duty to encourage her to speak and teach, as she has an opportunity, in all religious assemblies.

Resolved, That the same amount of virtue, delicacy, and refinement of behavior that is required of woman in the social state, should also be required of man, and the same transgressions should be visited with equal severity on both man and woman.

Resolved, That the objection of indelicacy and impropriety, which is so often brought against woman when she addresses a public audience, comes with a very ill-grace from those who encourage, by their attendance, her appearance on the stage, in the concert, or in feats of the circus.

Resolved, That woman has too long rested satisfied in the circumscribed limits which corrupt customs and a perverted application of the Scriptures have marked out for her, and that it is time she should move in the enlarged sphere which her great Creator has assigned her.

Resolved, That it is the duty of the women of this country to secure to themselves their sacred right to the elective franchise.

Resolved, That the equality of human rights results necessarily from the fact of the identity of the race in capabilities and responsibilities.

Resolved, therefore, That, being invested by the Creator with the same capabilities, and the same consciousness of responsibility for their exercise, it is demonstrably the right and duty of woman, equally with man, to promote every righteous cause by every righteous means; and especially in regard to the great subjects of morals and religion, it is self-evidently her right to participate with her brother in teaching them, both in private and in public, by writing and by speaking, by any instrumentalities proper to be used, and in any assemblies proper to be held; and this being a self-evident truth growing out of the divinely implanted principles of human nature, any custom or authority adverse to it, whether modern or wearing the hoary sanction of antiquity, is to be regarded as a self-evident falsehood, and at war with mankind.

At the last session Lucretia Mott offered and spoke to the following resolution:

Resolved, That the speedy success of our cause depends upon the zealous and untiring efforts of both men and women, for the overthrow of the monopoly of the pulpit, and for the securing to women an equal participation with men in the various trades, professions, and commerce.

DOCUMENT 2

Akron Convention, Akron, Ohio, May 28–29, 1851. Reminiscences by Frances D. Gage of Sojourner Truth

The leaders of the movement trembled on seeing a tall, gaunt black woman in a gray dress and white turban, surmounted with an uncouth sun-bonnet, march deliberately into the church, walk with the air of a queen up the aisle, and take her seat upon the pulpit steps. A buzz of disapprobation was heard all over the house, and there fell on the listening ear, "An abolition affair!" "Woman's rights and niggers!" "I told you so!" "Go it, darkey!"

I chanced on that occasion to wear my first laurels in public life as president of the meeting. At my request order was restored, and the business of the Convention went on. Morning, afternoon, and evening exercises came and went. Through all these sessions old Sojourner, quiet and reticent as the "Lybian Statue," sat crouched against the wall on the corner of the pulpit stairs, her sun-bonnet shading her eyes, her elbows on her knees, her chin resting upon her broad, hard palms. At intermission she was busy selling the "Life of Sojourner Truth," a narrative of her own strange and adventurous life. Again and again, timorous and trembling ones came to me and said, with earnestness, "Don't let her speak, Mrs. Gage, it will ruin us. Every newspaper in the land will have our cause mixed up with abolition and niggers, and we shall be utterly denounced." My only answer was, "We shall see when the time comes."

The second day the work waxed warm. Methodist, Baptist, Episcopal, Presbyterian, and Universalist ministers came in to hear and discuss the resolutions presented. One claimed superior rights and privileges for man, on the ground of "superior intellect"; another, because of the "manhood of Christ; if God had desired the equality of woman, He would have given some token of His will through the birth, life, and death of the Savior." Another gave us a theological view of the "sin of our first mother."

There were very few women in those days who dared to "speak in meeting"; and the august teachers of the

people were seemingly getting the better of us, while the boys in the galleries, and the sneerers among the pews, were hugely enjoying the discomfiture, as they supposed, of the "strong-minded." Some of the tender-skinned friends were on the point of losing dignity, and the atmosphere betokened a storm. When, slowly from her seat in the corner rose Sojourner Truth, who, till now, had scarcely lifted her head. "Don't let her speak!" gasped half a dozen in my ear. She moved slowly and solemnly to the front, laid her old bonnet at her feet, and turned her great speaking eyes to me. There was a hissing sound of disapprobation above and below. I rose and announced, "Sojourner Truth," and begged the audience to keep silence for a few moments.

The tumult subsided at once, and every eye was fixed on this almost Amazon form, which stood nearly six feet high, head erect, and eyes piercing the upper air like one in a dream. At her first word there was a profound hush. She spoke in deep tones, which, though not loud, reached every ear in the house, and away through the throng at the doors and windows.

"Wall, chilern, whar dar is so much racket dar must be somethin' out o' kilter. I tink dat 'twixt de niggers of de Souf and de womin at de Norf, all talkin' 'bout rights, de white men will be in a fix pretty soon. But what's all dis here talkin' 'bout?

"Dat man ober dar say dat womin needs to be helped into carriages, and lifted ober ditches, and to hab de best place everywhar. Nobody eber helps me into carriages, or ober mud-puddles, or gibs me any best place!" And raising herself to her full height, and her voice to a pitch like rolling thunder, she asked, "And a'n't I a woman? Look at me! Look at my arm! (and she bared her right arm to the shoulder, showing her tremendous muscular power). I have ploughed, and planted, and gathered into barns, and no man could head me! And a'n't I a woman? I could work as much and eat as much as a man—when I could get it—and bear de lash as well! And a'n't I a woman? I have borne thirteen chilern, and seen 'em mos' all sold off to slavery, and when I cried out with my mother's grief, none but Jesus heard me! And a'n't I a woman?

"Den dey talks 'bout dis ting in de head; what dis dey call it?" ("Intellect," whispered some one near.) "Dat's it, honey. What's dat got to do wid womin's rights? If my cup won't hold but a pint, and yourn holds a quart, wouldn't ye be mean not to let me have my little half-measure full?" And she pointed her significant finger, and sent a keen glance at the minister who had made the argument. The cheering was long and loud.

"Den dat little man in black dar, he say women can't have as much rights as men, 'cause Christ wan't a woman! Whar did your Christ come from?" Rolling thunder couldn't have stilled that crowd, as did those deep, wonderful tones, as she stood there with outstretched arms and eyes of fire. Raising her voice still louder, she repeated, "What did your Christ come from? From God and a woman! Man had nothin' to do wid Him." Oh, what a rebuke that was to that little man.

Turning again to another objector, she took up the defense of Mother Eve. I can not follow her through it all. It was pointed, and witty, and solemn; eliciting at almost every sentence deafening applause; and she ended by asserting: "If de fust woman God ever made was strong enough to turn de world upside down all alone, dese women togedder (and she glanced her eye over the

Source: Stanton, Elizabeth, Susan B. Anthony and Matilda J. Gage, eds., *History of Woman Suffrage* (Rochester, N.Y.: Fowler and Wells, 1881–1922, I, 115–116; reprint by Arno Press, 1969).

platform) ought to be able to turn it back, and get it right side up again! And now dey is asking to do it, de men better let 'em." Long-continued cheering greeted this. " 'Bleeged to ye for hearin' on me, and now ole Sojourner han't got nothin' more to say."

Amid roars of applause, she returned to her corner, leaving more than one of us with streaming eyes, and hearts beating with gratitude. She had taken us up in her strong arms and carried us safely over the slough of difficulty turning the whole tide in our favor. I have never in my life seen anything like the magical influence that subdued the mobbish spirit of the day, and turned the sneers and jeers of an excited crowd into notes of respect and admiration. Hundreds rushed up to shake hands with her, and congratulate the glorious old mother, and bid her God-speed on her mission of "testifyin' agin concerning the wickedness of this here people."

Chapter 2

Who Shall Vote in America?: The Post-Civil War Amendments to the Nineteenth Amendment

The Civil War and its aftermath had a deep effect on American feminism, just as it did on nearly all aspects of our political life. Some of the effects were organizational, affecting the structure of the movement and the political coalition backing women's rights. Closely related to these were shifts in emphasis concerning the theory or goals of the women's movement.

Anyone who has read Louisa May Alcott's *Little Women*, set during the Civil War years, remembers the picture of the March girls knitting washcloths for the Union Army, and young Jo longing for a broader sphere of action. Many women found such an outlet in the Sanitary Commission, which performed nursing services, maintained hospital ships, established relief camps, and conducted campaigns for adequate sanitation and nutrition for the Union army. Such work, moreover, developed sophisticated organizational skills in women, even in those who had not previously been interested in activity beyond their home responsibilities. Smaller than the Sanitary Commission but nonetheless important in politicizing women was the National Women's Loyal League, founded by Elizabeth Cady Stanton and Susan B. Anthony in 1863. The National Women's Loyal League pledged itself to work for the abolition of slavery and petitioned for the adoption of the Thirteenth Amendment to the U.S. Constitution, which abolished slavery. (The Emancipation Proclamation had only freed slaves in areas in rebellion against the Union.) The work of the Loyal League was directly related to the abolitionism of the first feminists; even in 1863 abolitionism was considered radical and dangerous to Republican electoral fortunes. The politics of the Loyal League were not only uncompromising with respect to slavery but clearly feminist as well. The summons to the founding meeting declared that:

> Woman is equally interested and responsible with man in the settlement of this final problem of self-government; therefore let none stand idle spectators now.

At the founding meeting, Anthony presented a resolution stating that there would be no true peace until the "civil and political rights of all citizens of African descent and all women" were practically established. This linking of women's rights and black liberation did not lead, unfortunately, to a lasting alliance between white women and blacks.

Women's work to affect black rights and the postwar political settlement produced enormous strain on the abolitionist-feminist coalition. Stanton and Anthony argued for the end of slavery on the grounds that it was both immoral and unjust to buy or sell any human being, that the "inalienable right" not to be deprived of "life, liberty, or the pursuit of happiness" was hopelessly violated by a slaveholding society. Similarly, when the war was over, they supported the enfranchisement of the freedmen, arguing that the consent of the governed upon which civil liberty depended could not exist without the vote. Both the abolitionists and most of the Republican Party agreed. But Stanton and Anthony took the argument one step further and pointed out that by the same logic women had a right to the vote, and that any Constitutional Amendment extending the franchise to the black male should also confer suffrage on women. Most abolitionists and Radical Republicans agreed with the logic of this argument but rejected it as inexpedient, in fact as politically impossible.

In 1866 Stanton and Anthony, along with Lucy Stone, Lucretia Mott and others formed the American Equal Rights Association, whose object was to combine the demand for black suffrage with that for woman suffrage by advocating universal adult suffrage. "Has not the time come to bury the black man and the woman in the citizen?" Stanton asked at the opening convention. (DuBois, 1981, 90) AERA's first campaign was against the wording of the proposed Fourteenth Amendment, which sought to protect freedmen's votes by stipulating that any state which did not allow all its "male citizens' to vote would have its congressional representation cut proportionately. AERA strongly protested the introduction of the word "male" into the Constitution. But even the Radical Republicans, fearful that the support for black suffrage would be undermined if it were associated with woman suffrage, refused to endorse AERA's petitions. After passage of the Fourteenth Amendment it became clear that the Congress would refuse to link black male suffrage and woman suffrage in any constitutional amendment; in the face of this political fact the feminists split into two camps. One group, under the leadership of Lucy Stone and Henry Blackwell, advocated accepting the priority of black male suffrage and the promises of radicals that they would work for woman suffrage once freedmen's rights were granted.

7

Frederick Douglass, too, reluctantly accepted the necessity of recognizing that this was "the Negro's hour," and of working later for women's enfranchisement. The other group, headed by Stanton and Anthony, opposed the ratification of the Fourteenth and Fifteenth Amendments in the name of women's rights, contending that it was wrong to give black males pecedence over black and white women.

The split in the AERA was both a personal and a political misfortune. Stanton and Anthony felt betrayed by those whom they had regarded as personal friends and close political allies. I am aware of no historian who has carefully analyzed the question of whether a firm commitment by the Republic Party could have carried woman suffrage along with black male enfranchisement. The general view is that most Republicans were simply uninterested in the issue of votes for women, while old abolitionists felt that they would not be able to carry both issues and that the need of the black male was more acute than that of women, often ignoring the existence of black women and their need for the ballot.

The bitter legacy of the campaign over the Fourteenth and Fifteenth Amendments not only divided Stanton and Anthony from their long-standing allies, but it goaded them and others to make racist assertions that white women should vote before ignorant and brutal black men. Stanton was especially prone to making anti-black utterances during the 1869 debates over ratification of the Fifteenth Amendment, which prohibited withholding suffrage on the basis of race but not sex. While her anger subsequently subsided, the habit of viewing woman's suffrage as a particular concern of middle class white women and of pitting women against other politically disadvantaged groups persisted, breaking forth at the turn of the century in anti-immigrant as well as anti-black rhetoric.

The defeat of woman suffrage in the post-Civil War Amendments also encouraged the formation of a more autonomous women's movement. Stanton's and Anthony's sense of betrayal spurred them to more militant and independent activities. They published a women's rights newspaper, *The Revolution*, which published articles on a wide range of radical issues such as divorce, marriage, reform, cooperative housekeeping, prostitution, and the low wages and economic exploitation of working-class women. In this sense the result of the Reconstruction battles was a return to the broadly-defined—though less politically sophisticated and radical—feminism of Seneca Falls.

Losing the battles over the Fourteenth and Fifteenth amendments intensified feminists' desire for the vote. In the 1870s they made a serious effort to procure the franchise without having to go through all the effort to win yet another constitutional amendment. The National Women's Suffrage Association, formed by Stanton and Anthony after the break-up of the AERA, adopted the argument that women were already enfranchised by the Constitution. Under the Fourteenth Amendment all citizens were to be protected in the exercise of the privileges of citizenship. If suffrage were a right of citizenship, under the Fourteenth and Fifteenth Amendments women already were entitled to vote. The AERA encouraged women around the country to take what was their right without further ado, and to vote in the elections of 1871 and 1872. Susan Anthony herself cast a ballot in Rochester in 1872, but was later arrested for this act of "illegal voting" and brought to trial. She defended herself by appeal to the equal and inalienable natural rights of all citizens. [See Document 3.] She lost her case, and due to a technicality was barred from appealing the decision, to her great disappointment. In 1875, however, the Supreme Court did rule on the question of whether the Fourteenth and Fifteenth Amendments had enfranchised women. In *Minor v. Happersett* the Court held that suffrage was not a right of citizenship but a privilege which states were free to grant to those they deemed fit. [See Document 4.] This defeat for woman suffrage marked the end of feminists' hopes that Reconstruction and the climate of political reform of the immediate postwar years would bring women as well as freedmen the vote.

Long years of trying to procure the vote for women either through passage of a federal constitutional amendment, or through amending state constitutions to allow woman suffrage, followed. Between 1870 and 1910, 480 state campaigns were held in thirty-three states, trying to get the issue submitted to the voters. Only seventeen resulted in actual referenda, and of these, only two (in Colorado and Idaho) were successful. (Flexner, 1959, 222) Despite this discouraging record, by the end of 1913 nine states, all west of the Mississippi River, had granted women full suffrage, while the Illinois legislature had granted women the vote in Presidential elections. (Flexner, 1959, 260–61)

In their efforts to gain support, suffrage leaders sometimes adopted tactics which drove a wedge between native-born white women and blacks and immigrants, both male and female. Even Susan B. Anthony who was in her personal life a staunch anti-racist, asked Frederick Douglass not to attend the meeting of the National American Women's Suffrage Association (NAWSA) when it met in Atlanta, Georgia, in order not to hinder the recruitment of southern white women. In 1893 NAWSA passed a resolution which read:

> Resolved: That without expressing any opinion on the proper qualifications for voting, we call attention to the significant facts that in every State there are more women who can read and write than the whole number of illiterate male voters; more white women who can read and write than all negro voters; more American women who can read and write than all foreign voters; so that the enfranchisement of such women would settle the vexed question of rule by illiteracy, whether of home-grown or foreign-born production. (quoted in Davis, 1981, 115–116)

The resolution not only played on racist fears, but ignored the needs and claims of black and immigrant women. At the 1899 NAWSA convention, Lottie Wilson Jackson, a black suffragist from Michigan (one of the few states with integrated chapters), who had had to ride in a segregated railroad car to attend the convention, moved a resolution stating "That colored women ought not to be compelled to ride in smoking cars, and that suitable accomodations should be provided for them." The resolution was defeated following Anthony's remark that "We women are a helpless and disfranchised class. Our hands are tied. While we are in this condition, it is not for us to go passing resolutions against the railroad corporations or anybody else." (quoted in Davis, 1981, 118) The last years of the nineteenth century form a dismal chapter in the suffrage effort—few practical gains were made, and many principles central to feminism's commitment to universal human rights were compromised or abandoned on the grounds of expediency.

The first years of the twentieth century saw scant progress towards women's suffrage, and that along with the enormous expenditure of time and energy in state campaigns spurred some suffrage workers to espouse more dramatic tactics than the national and state organizations had so far used. In 1913, on the eve of Woodrow Wilson's inauguration, two young women recently appointed to the Congressional Committee of the National American Women's Suffrage Association (NAWSA), Alice Paul and Lucy Burns, staged a suffrage parade of 5,000 women. The parade generated great publicity, not only because of the large number of marchers, but also because the police failed to maintain order in the crowd of hostile onlookers. Near-riots broke out at places along the route, shocking many and focusing national attention on suffrage. After the suffrage parade, Alice Paul employed increasingly dramatic tactics to advance the suffrage cause: an automobile procession to the Capitol carrying a petition of 200,000 signatures; publication of a weekly newspaper, *The Suffragist*; and in 1917, picketing in front of the White House and engaging in hunger strikes after being arrested. Paul's militant style and her refusal to work for any measures other than a federal amendment were incompatible with the NAWSA's policies of working for state referenda as well as a federal amendment and of working within the law. In 1914 Paul's organization (now called the Congressional Union, and after 1916 the National Woman's Party) split from the NAWSA.

In the meantime, however, the NAWSA itself had become revitalized. Under the leadership of Carrie Chapman Catt, who assumed the presidency in 1916, the NAWSA began a well-orchestrated campaign which worked both for a federal amendment and for suffrage referenda in carefully selected states. U.S. entry into World War I aided the suffrage movement. Both the Woman's Party and NAWSA pointed out the discrepancy of fighting for democracy and self-determination abroad while denying women the vote at home. NAWSA endorsed the war effort, and emphasized women's contributions to that cause. In 1917 President Wilson, a convert to the suffrage cause, asked Congress to pass a women's suffrage amendment because such a measure was "vital to the winning of the war." (quoted in Woloch, 1984, 353) In 1917, North Dakota, Ohio, Indiana, Rhode Island, Nebraska and Michigan granted women presidential suffrage by legislative action (although in Indiana and Ohio these actions were later cancelled), and most importantly a woman's suffrage referendum won in New York State. (Flexner, 1959, 290) The New York victory was particularly significant because the state was so large and the electoral victory was the first in an eastern industrial state.

It took another year-and-a-half, however, to get the federal amendment through Congress. The House approved the measure on May 20 and the Senate on June 4, 1919. These congressional votes were followed by a grueling ratification campaign, and it frequently appeared that the amendment would fail. However, in August, 1920, the Tennessee legislature became the thirty-sixth to ratify the amendment, and despite subsequent actions by die-hard "antis" challenging this and other ratifications in court, women voted in the elections of November, 1920.

Organizations dedicated to woman suffrage had to work a full half-century after the Civil War before women were enfranchised throughout the country. Although in the immediate post-Civil War years their failure can be attributed in part to the burning issues of Reconstruction and protection for the freedman, the prolonged struggle after 1900 reveals the depth of opposition to woman suffrage itself. The "anti" literature of these years is filled with the most blatant, as well as more subtle, misogynism. Women were depicted as too ignorant, too emotional, and sometimes as biologically incapable of using the vote rationally and responsibly. Antis also insisted that women's place was in the home, and that going to the polling place was but the first step away from their domestic duties. Suffragists responded with a range of arguments. Women had a natural and inalienable right to the vote. Women needed the vote in order to help clean up city government, procure safe streets, and provide sanitary food and water; and, in seeking the franchise, women were only seeking to fulfill their traditional responsibility of providing a healthy environment for their families. Most perniciously some suffragists argued that Yankee women needed the vote to help their men control colored and immigrant populations.

Some scholars have argued that the intensity of the last phases of the struggle for suffrage not only led to the adoption of bad arguments on both sides, but that the last phases of the struggle for suffrage narrowed the focus of American feminism from the broad agenda of divorce reform, domestic relations, education, employment and the sexual double-standard to a single-issue campaign. (e.g. O'Neill, 1969; Chafe, 1972) As a consequence, they assert, once the vote was won feminism was eclipsed by other movements and issues. Yet more was at stake in the suffrage battle than simply women's right to cast a vote. To some extent suffrage came to symbolize women's responsibilities to a world beyond the home, and the possibility of their moving into the public realm. (DuBois, 1975) The bitterness and intensity of the opposition to woman suffrage reveals how many people sought to maintain the idea that men and women occupy, and should continue to occupy, quite separate spheres. While women have now exercised the right to vote for more than sixty years, the question of women's proper role in public and political life, and of men's responsibility for domestic life, is far from resolved.

DOCUMENT 3

Account of the Proceedings on the Trial of Susan B. Anthony on the Charge of Illegal Voting at the Presidential Election in November, 1872

JUDGE HUNT: (Ordering the defendant to stand up), Has the prisoner anything to say why sentence shall not be pronounced?

MISS ANTHONY: Yes, your honor, I have many things to say; for in your ordered verdict of guilty, you have trampled under foot every vital principle of our government. My natural rights, my civil rights, my political rights, my judicial rights, are all alike ignored. Robbed of the fundamental privilege of citizenship, I am degraded from the status of a citizen to that of a subject; and not only myself individually, but all of my sex, are, by your honor's verdict, doomed to political subjection under this, so-called, form of government.

JUDGE HUNT: The Court cannot listen to a rehearsal of arguments the prisoner's counsel has already consumed three hours in presenting.

MISS ANTHONY: May it please your honor, I am not arguing the question, but simply stating the reasons why

Source: Koedt, Anne, Ellen Levine, Anita Rapone, eds., *Radical Feminism* (New York: Quadrangle Books, 1973), 17–19.

sentence cannot, in justice, be pronounced against me. Your denial of my citizen's right to vote, is the denial of my right of consent as one of the governed, the denial of my right of representation as one of the taxed, the denial of my right to a trial by a jury of my peers as an offender against law, therefore, the denial of my sacred rights to life, liberty, property and—

JUDGE HUNT: The Court cannot allow the prisoner to go on.

MISS ANTHONY: But your honor will not deny me this one and only poor privilege of protest against this high-handed outrage upon my citizen's rights. May it please the Court to remember that since the day of my arrest last November, this is the first time that either myself or any person of my disfranchised class has been allowed a word of defense before judge or jury—

JUDGE HUNT: The prisoner must sit down—the Court cannot allow it.

MISS ANTHONY: All of my prosecutors, from the 8th ward corner grocery politician, who entered the complaint, to the United States Marshal, Commissioner, District Attorney, District Judge, your honor on the bench, not one is my peer, but each and all are my political sovereigns; and had your honor submitted my case to the jury, as was clearly your duty, even then I should have had just cause of protest, for not one of those men was my peer; but, native or foreign born, white or black, rich or poor, educated or ignorant, awake or asleep, sober or drunk, each and every man of them was my political superior; hence, in no sense, my peer. Even, under such circumstances, a commoner of England, tried before a jury of Lords, would have far less cause to complain than should I, a woman, tried before a jury of men. Even my counsel, the Hon. Henry R. Selden, who has argued my cause to ably, so earnestly, so unanswerably before your honor, is my political sovereign. Precisely as no disfranchised person is entitled to sit upon a jury, and no woman is entitled to the franchise, so, none but a regularly admitted lawyer is allowed to practice in the courts, and no woman can gain admission to the bar—hence, jury, judge, counsel, must all be of the superior class.

JUDGE HUNT: The Court must insist—the prisoner has been tried according to the established forms of law.

MISS ANTHONY: Yes, your honor, but by forms of law all made by men, interpreted by men, administered by men, in favor of men, and against women; and hence, your honor's ordered verdict of guilty, against a United States citizen for the exercise of *"that citizen's right to vote,"* simply because that citizen was a woman and not a man. But, yesterday, the same manmade forms of law, declared it a crime punishable with $1,000 fine and six months' imprisonment, for you, or me, or any of us, to give a cup of cold water, a crust of bread, or a night's shelter to a panting fugitive as he was tracking his way to Canada. And every man or woman in whose veins coursed a drop of human sympathy violated that wicked law, reckless of consequences, and was justified in so doing. As then, the slaves who got their freedom must take it over, or under, or through the unjust forms of law, precisely so, now, must women, to get their right to a voice in this government, take it; and I have taken mine, and mean to take it at every possible opportunity.

JUDGE HUNT: The Court orders the prisoner to sit down. It will not allow another word.

MISS ANTHONY: When I was brought before your honor for trial, I hoped for a broad and liberal interpretation of the Constitution and its recent amendments, one that should declare all United States citizens under its protecting aegis—that should declare equality of rights the national guarantee to all persons born or naturalized in the United States. But failing to get this justice—failing, even, to get a trial by a jury *not* of my peers—I ask not leniency at your hands—but rather the full rigors of the law.

JUDGE HUNT: The Court must insist—

(Here the prisoner sat down.)

JUDGE HUNT: The prisoner will stand up.

(Here Miss Anthony arose again.)

The sentence of the Court is that you pay a fine of one hundred dollars and the costs of the prosecution.

MISS ANTHONY: May it please your honor, I shall never pay a dollar of your unjust penalty. All the stock in trade I possess is a $10,000 debt, incurred by publishing my paper—*The Revolution*—four years ago, the sole object of which was to educate all women to do precisely as I have done, rebel against your manmade, unjust, unconstitutional forms of law, that tax, fine, imprison and hang women, while they deny them the right of representation in the government; and I shall work on with might and main to pay every dollar of that honest debt, but not a penny shall go to this unjust claim. And I shall earnestly and persistently continue to urge all women to the practical recognition of the old revolutionary maxim, that "Resistance to tyranny is obedience to God."

JUDGE HUNT: Madam, the Court will not order you committed until the fine is paid.

DOCUMENT 4

Virginia L. Minor, and Francis Minor v. Reese Happersett (1875) 21 Wall. 162

MR. CHIEF JUSTICE WAITE delivered the opinion of the Court.

The question is presented in this case, whether, since the adoption of the Fourteenth amendment, a woman, who is a citizen, of the United States and of the State of Missouri, is a voter in that State, notwithstanding the provision of the constitution and laws of the State, which confine the right to suffrage to men alone. . . .

It is contended that the provisions of the constitution and laws of the State of Missouri which confine the right of suffrage and registration therefore to men, are in violation of the Constitution of the United States and, therefore, void. The argument is, that as a woman, born and naturalized in the United States and subject to the jurisdiction thereof, is a citizen of the United States and of the State in which she resides, she has the right of suffrage as one of the privileges and immunities of her citizenship, which the State cannot by its laws or Constitution abridge.

There is no doubt that women may be citizens. They are persons, and by the Fourteenth Amendment "All persons born or naturalized in the United States and subject to the jurisdiction thereof" are expressly declared to be "citizens of the United States and of the State wherein they reside". . . .

If the right of suffrage is one of the necessary privileges of a citizen of the United States, then the Constitution and laws of Missouri confining it to men are in violation of the Constitution of the United States, as amended, and conse-

Source: *Minor* v. *Happersett* (1875) 21 Wall. 162.

quently void. The direct question is, therefore, presented whether all citizens are necessarily voters. . . .

It is clear . . . we think, that the Constitution has not added the right of suffrage to the privileges and immunities of citizenship as they existed at the time it was adopted. This makes it proper to inquire whether suffrage was co-extensive with the citizenship of the States at the time of its adoption. If it was, then it may with force be argued that suffrage was one of the rights which belonged to citizenship, and in the enjoyment of which every citizen must be protected. But if it was not, the contrary may with propriety be assumed.

[It is shown that suffrage was not enjoyed by all citizens at the time of the adoption of the constitution.]

[Further,] by the very terms of the Amendment we have been considering (the fourteenth), "Representatives shall be apportioned among the several States according to their respective numbers, counting the whole number of persons in each State, excluding Indians not taxed. But when the right to vote at any election for the choice of electors for President and Vice-President of the United States, representatives in Congress, the executive and judicial officers of a State, or the member of the Legislature thereof, is denied to any of the male inhabitants of such State, being twenty-one years of age and citizens of the United States, or in any way abridged, except for participation in the rebellion, or other crimes, the basis of representation therein shall be reduced in the proportion which the number of such male citizens shall bear to the whole number of male citizens twenty-one years of age in such State." Why this, if it was not in the power of the Legislature to deny the right of suffrage to some male inhabitants? And if suffrage was necessarily one of the absolute rights of citizenship, why confine the operation of the limitation to male inhabitants? Women and children are, as we have seen, "persons." They are counted in the enumeration upon which the appropriation is to be made, but if they were necessarily voters because of their citizenship unless clearly excluded, why inflict the penalty for the exclusion of males alone? Clearly, no such form of words would have been selected to express the idea here indicated, if suffrage was the absolute right of all citizens.

And still again; after the adoption of the Fourteenth Amendment, it was deemed necessary to adopt a fifteenth, as follows: "The right of citizens of the United States to vote shall not be denied or abridged by the United States, or by any State, on account of race, color or previous condition of servitude." The Fourteenth Amendment had already provided that no State should make or enforce any law which should abridge the privileges or immunities of citizens of the United States. If suffrage was one of these privileges or immunities, why amend the Constitution to prevent its being denied on account of race, etc.? Nothing is more evident than that the greater must include the less, and if all were already protected, why go through with the form of amending the Constitution to protect a part? . . . .

Certainly, if the courts can consider any question settled, this is one. For nearly ninety years the people have acted upon the idea that the constitution, when it conferred citizenship, did not necessarily confer the right of suffrage. If uniform practice, long continued, can settle the construction of so important an instrument as the Constitution of the United States confessedly is, most certainly it has been done here. Our province is to decide what the law is, not to declare what it should be. . . .

Being unanimously of the opinion that the Constitution of the United States does not confer the right of suffrage upon anyone, and that the Constitutions and laws of the several States which commit that important trust to men alone are not necessarily void, we *Affirm* the judgment of the court below.

CHAPTER 3

Women's Welfare vs. Women's Rights, 1890–1930: Temperance, Anti-Lynching, and Protective Labor Legislation

Suffrage was by no means the only issue which occupied American feminists in the late nineteenth century and early twentieth centuries. Those interested in women's welfare worked in a variety of causes which greatly expanded the number of women engaged in public work, the number and size of the organizations to which they belonged, and the definition of what women needed to share fully in America's promise of political freedom and material abundance. It is impossible here to analyze fully the range of thought and activity of the period, but three campaigns of great importance—temperance, anti-lynching, and protective labor legislation—indicate the broad scope of feminist ideology and political activity.

A. Temperance

Temperance had been a "woman's issue" as early as the 1850s. As noted in Chapter 1, Susan Anthony began her public work as a temperance organizer, linking temperance with women's need for the ballot and the right to divorce. In the 1870s temperance reemerged as a political issue, and temperance organizations grew rapidly in number and influence. By 1900 the women's Christian Temperance Union (WCTU) had 176,000 members in over 7,000 locals, and was the largest women's organization to that time in the United States. (Epstein, 1980, 120) In 1919 the Eighteenth Amendment prohibited the manufacture and sale of liquor in the United States, and Prohibition lasted until 1933.

The temperance movement was initiated not by women but by Protestant men (largely Congregationalists) interested in sobriety, moral reform, and respectability. Temperance soon attracted women who were similarly interested in moral reform, and others who were consciously or unconsciously angered by their subordinate status within the home. Increasingly relegated to domestic concerns by the ideology of the home and the movement of productive employment out of the household, women found a growing divergence between the largely male worlds of education, employment and production and women's domestic life. This separation evoked a complex response from women. On the one hand women asserted that they had a particular responsibility for the home; in the late nineteenth century the WCTU adopted as its slogan, "Home Protection." On the other hand, women

insisted that they now needed to act in the public sphere if they were to fulfill their obligations to their families. If women were to protect the sanctity of home life from the profligacy of drunken husbands and the bar-room, they needed not only moral persuasion but the ballot in order to revoke liquor laws and close the saloons, to insure police protection and safe streets, and to establish schools and kindergartens for proper moral education. Hence in many instances the interests of feminists such as Susan Anthony who were fighting for women's political equality, and temperance workers whose primary interest was moral reform and defense of the home, converged in the demand for the ballot and public activity by women. (Although not part of the temperance literature *per se*, see Jane Addams' very effective argument for women in city government, Document 5.)

Frances Willard (1839–1898), president of the WCTU from 1879 until her death, brought together feminist and moral reform concerns. The main temperance arguments concerning female victimization were that men who drank spent money on liquor which should have gone to maintain the home. Such men were likely to lose their jobs, perhaps forcing wife and children to work, they spent time in the saloon which should have been spent with their families, and they were likely to be brutal and violent. There was class as well as sex antagonism in the women's assault on drink. They often portrayed working-class immigrant men as the worst drinkers, and the most stubborn in their opposition to temperance. The call for purer, safer, cleaner homes was thus particularly directed at the working class. This had some positive effects; Willard's reformist impulses, for example, led her to espouse a "living wage" and the eight-hour day, among other measures.

The temperance movement was linked to feminism by its advocacy of women's suffrage and by its encouragement of women to develop responsibility and power. The WCTU told women that they had the right to demand from men the same conduct in sexual relations and in everyday social life that was expected of women. It encouraged women to exert equal control with their husbands over their sexual lives, and to decide themselves when they would bear children. The temperance ideal of "social purity" has popularly been ridiculed as Victorian prudery. (This ridicule has itself served as a way of putting women in their place.) Along with undoubted elements of sexual repression, however, was a sharp insight that sex could be an important area of conflict between men and women, and that nineteenth century women "were made subordinate to and dependent upon men in sexual activity and through pregnancy and childbirth." (Epstein, 1980, 128) The WCTU's attitude toward sex as well as toward drink was in many respects politically astute.

There are problems in calling the WCTU a "feminist" organization, despite the fact that it mobilized women on a major scale and gave many of them a new sense of their social responsibilities and their capabilities. The WCTU did support women's rights and women's equality, but it also sanctioned conventional morality and women's traditional responsibility for the home. At bottom women's equality and the ideals of "Home Protection" were incompatible. Conventional morality and traditional understandings of home life supported a male-dominated family structure, not sexual equality. Since the home was the only place women were accorded real authority, it was understandable that they became its fervant guardians. Ultimately, however, women's equality would require not only the vote but a reordering of family life to make it less exclusively "women's sphere." Few women in the nineteenth century were ready to take such a step.

B. Anti-Lynching

Opposition to lynching, like opposition to drink, was not self-evidently a feminist issue, yet it also politicized many women and implicitly criticized the sexual "balance of power." Ida B. Wells (1869–1931) was one of those who spurred the anti-lynching campaign. Wells, orphaned at age 16, was first a teacher and then an editor of the Memphis *Free Speech* in Tennessee. In 1892 the *Free Speech* was destroyed by a mob after Wells denounced the lynching of three black men. Their deaths, she said, were the result of the success of their grocery store which cut into the business of a white-owned store. Wells, who was in Philadelphia when the press was destroyed, was warned not to return to Memphis or she would herself be lynched. Wells' response was to launch a crusade againt lynching through other newspapers, lecture platforms, and publication of her book, *The Red Record*, a book which compiled accounts and statistics about lynching.

The radical core of Wells' argument was that lynching was not simply the result of occasional lawlessness, but an integral part of a system of racial oppression. The statistics she gathered were horrifying: since the end of the Civil War 10,000 Blacks had been killed by mobs, and only three white men convicted and executed for these murders. Furthermore, Wells demonstrated that the motives for lynching were usually political or economic, as in the Memphis case. This flew in the face of the commonly accepted belief that lynching was a response to rape. According to this view, crowds of white men were carried away by the passion of the moment upon learning of the assault of a black man upon a white woman; not waiting for the slow wheels of justice, they executed the culprit on the spot. The extent to which this scenario had taken hold of the public mind is reflected in Jane Addams' condemnation of lynching. [See Document 6.] Addams' essay was a brave and important denunciation of lynching—brave because it was not seemly for women to speak of rape, and important because of Addams' prestige and influence in Progressive circles. Yet as Ida Wells' reply to Addams points out, even though Addams condemned lynching as

inexcusable, she regarded it as a response to inter-racial rape. [See Document 7.] Racial stereotypes clouded the thinking of even independent thinkers like Addams.

In addition to uncovering the vast extent of lynching and debunking the myth that it was a response to rape, Wells also analyzed the mutually reinforcing aspects of sexual and racial oppression. She spoke openly of the systematic sexual exploitation black women suffered under slavery. She showed how the notion that black women were "loose"—a widespread prejudice in nineteenth century America—reflected the fact that black women were defenseless against their white masters under slavery, and was now a means of keeping black women in their place. She saw the defense of black women's reputations as part of a larger campaign against attitudes which kept all members of the race vulnerable to abuse and terror. She also refuted the notion that every sexual encounter between a black man and a white woman must be rape. Many of these liaisons, she asserted, were based on *mutual* attraction and not infrequently when the woman's family discovered the liaison, they cried "rape," rather than acknowledge that a white woman might love a black man.

Wells showed how the strong power of sexual fantasies and fears were used to reinforce racial oppression. Black women were labelled immoral, which helped to restrict their activities. Black men were caricatured as lustful brutes whose sexual passions threatened the safety of white women and the sanctity of the home. The fact that the mob was called out when black men asserted themselves politically or economically showed how sexual stereotypes could be put to the use of much broader political and social subjection. And while Wells' major concern was the plight of black people, her analysis showed that the pressure not only to *be* "pure" but to *appear* pure hampered *every* woman's freedom of movement, friendships with men, and ability to take part in public life.

Wells' anti-lynching campaign sparked the formation of black women's clubs, which in turn served as important vehicles for the further politicization of black women. On the eve of Wells' departure for an anti-lynching lecture tour in England, Victoria Earle Matthews of New York and Susan McKinney of Brooklyn were inspired to form the women's Loyal Union in New York, and a little later Mrs. Josephine St. Pierre Ruffin of Boston formed the New Era Club. Ida B. Wells began a women's club in Chicago in 1893, and others sprang up in major urban centers. Despite the overlap between their goals, black and white women's clubs remained largely, although not universally, segregated. In 1900, Mary Church Terrell, representing the National Association of Colored Women, was denied a seat at the convention of the General Federation of Women's Clubs. Josephine St. Pierre Ruffin was offered a seat as a representative of the predominantly white women's club to which she belonged, but was turned away when she insisted upon sitting as a representative of the Women's Era Club, a black organization. (Woloch, 1984, 292; Lerner, 1972, 447–450) Black women's clubs did anti-lynching work, founded kindergartens, established settlement houses and shelters from prostitution rings for young black women recently up from the South, sponsored education lectures, and developed stands on local issues affecting the black community. Most supported women's suffrage for the additional tool it would give black women in their community work. In 1900 Fannie Barrier Williams, who had been excluded from a white women's club in Chicago, described the impetus for the black women's club movement: "Among colored women . . . the club is only one of many means for the social uplift of a race. Among white women the club is the onward movement of the already uplifted. . . ." Most black women's clubs similarly conceived of their activities as being undertaken not only on behalf of women alone, but of the entire black community.

Some feminists have criticized the tradition of black women giving as much attention as they did to the advancement of black men. But as Wells' writings make clear, the vulnerability of the black male terrorized black women as well. Black women, as members of a subject class, confronted a complex of problems only some of which they shared with white women on account of their sex, others which white women were spared as members of the dominant race. The experiences and testimony of nineteenth century black women clearly illustrate the fact that the nature of sex oppression is not universal, but varies with class, race, and cultural heritage.

C. Protective Legislation and Equal Rights

Women's trade union activity and debates over protective labor legislation and the proposed Equal Rights Amendment of 1923 provide a third vantage point from which to view the complexity of "the first wave" of American feminism. The National Women's Trade Union League (WTUL) was founded in 1903, partly as a result of the failure of the American Federation of Labor or its affiliates actively to organize women. The impetus for the WTUL came both from working-class women who somehow found the energy, time and education to become organizers, and from middle class feminists concerned with the betterment of women.

The WTUL organized women workers into unions; helped plan, fund (albeit on the most meager of resources), and carry out strikes; encouraged educational activities; and helped lead the battle for protective labor legislation. Such legislation included mandatory rest periods during the day, the provision of chairs or stools for department store clerks, higher standards of sanitation, and other measures to ameliorate the conditions under which women worked. But the WTUL's primary concern was maximum hours and minimum wages legislation. These were, of course, goals for the labor movement as a whole, but in 1905 in *Lochner* vs. *New York* the Supreme Court had ruled that maximum hours legislation, and by analogy other regulations of the terms of work like minimum wage legislation, was an unconstitutional violation of freedom of contract between worker and employer. In response to the *Lochner* decision, labor leaders and members of the WTUL and the National Consumers' League (a powerful, largely middle-class organization founded in the 1890s for improving working conditions) began to work for protective legislation for women, reasoning that the Court might accord the "weaker sex" protection it was unwilling to grant to men. In 1908 the National Consumers' League prepared a brief for lawyer Louis Brandeis on the basis of which the Supreme Court upheld Oregon's maximum hours law for women working in factories, laundries, or other "mechanical establishments." *Muller* v. *Oregon* [see Document 8] was a pathbreaking case: the "Brandeis brief" was the first to use sociological data and statistics as part of its legal argument. *Muller* v. *Oregon* was hailed by liberals as a victory for labor. Maximum hours legislation would extend to

women, who were notoriously difficult to organize, the kinds of concessions which men won through unionization and collective bargaining. Moreover, it was the first chink in the armor of "freedom of contract" (which amounted to freedom mainly for the employer). Finally, in some instances when employers had to provide a benefit to women, they extended it to men as well.

Most feminists in the early years of the twentieth century supported protective legislation for women, seeing it as crucial to ensure the dignity and well-being of working-class women. Since women formed the backbone of many of the lobbying groups, the victories of passing protective legislation and winning the *Muller* case before the Supreme Court were indications of women's growing political sophistication and power.

Nonetheless, particularly after women obtained the vote, some feminists launched an attack on protective legislation for women. They did not object to government regulation of industry, but argued that any provisions concerning hours and conditions of work should apply to men and women equally. They pointed out that some of the assumptions embedded in *Muller* v. *Oregon* were inimical to women's long-term interests. Brandeis had argued that women needed protective legislation not only because women were weaker than men, but also because women who worked strained their bodies and their nervous systems and were prone to bear unhealthy children. This kind of reasoning had the potential of being turned against women. Since women were weak and were potential mothers they should be *excluded* from some jobs, not just protected from overwork, and they could be barred from overtime and prevented from earning the extra wages men could draw.

Attention to women's maternal functions, however, could also be used to women's advantage. In 1912 the Department of Labor established the Children's Bureau and a few years later the Women's Bureau. Both gave women unprecedented opportunity for government work, and to press for legislation endorsed by women's groups: prohibition of child labor, compulsory education, unemployment compensation, mothers' pensions, and the much-acclaimed Sheppard-Towner Act of 1921. The Sheppard-Towner Act was the first federally-funded health care act, and provided money for prenatal and child health centers. Ironically, while arguments about women's maternal duties and nature had been used by anti-suffragists to keep women from the vote, "social feminists" of the early twentieth century pointed to the special needs of mothers in order to procure government aid for women and children, particularly for working women and their families. As the next chapter shows, much of the impetus for the welfare legislation of the New Deal originated in the ideas and activities of these women.

By the 1920s a significant split had developed within feminist ranks between the social feminists who supported a wide range of legislation to improve women's welfare, and members of the National Women's Party (NWP) who opposed all legislation based on sex. In 1923 the National Women's Party introduced in Congress an Equal Rights Amendment which stated that "men and women shall have equal rights throughout the United States and every place subject to its jurisdiction." The National Consumers' League, the WTUL, the League of Women Voters, and the General Federation of Women's Clubs all strongly *opposed* the ERA. While they wanted to get rid of women's legal disabilities and wanted to open professional opportunities to women, they thought that factory and other working-class women needed the protection of the state. There was thus a deep ideological division within the ranks of American feminists with respect to the issue of equal rights. In 1930 *Equal Rights*, the newspaper of the National Women's Party, published an account of hearings held on a proposed New York State statute which would have exempted women restaurant workers from protective legislation prohibiting night work for women. The National Women's Party supported this legislation as a step toward eliminating protective legislation for women; the WTUL and the National Consumers' League opposed it. The major positions on both sides are well-captured in the article. [See Document 9.]

The debate between the early supporters of an Equal Rights Amendment and "social feminists" is of more than simply historical interest. It raised the difficult and complex question of what constitutes "equality" between men and women. In the 1920s women activists worried that equal treatment under the law would in practice work to women's disadvantage, forcing non-unionized, poorly paid, unskilled women to work under the most brutal conditions, while unionized male workers would be in a position to bargain with their employers. In the 1970s virtually all feminists came to support the ERA, but significant numbers argued that the ERA held out a false hope of rectifying women's secondary status in American society. Genuine equality would require deep changes in values and attitudes, new structures of work, and the involvement of both men and women in child-rearing.

By the early years of the twentieth century American feminism had developed fairly sophisticated analyses of the causes and effects of sexual inequality. Drawing on the Enlightenment tradition, feminists had argued that women must be considered men's intellectual, moral, and political equals. They put forward a partial critique of the doctrine of separate spheres, asserting that women could not "by nature" be confined to the world of domesticity. (Few, however, concluded that men should shoulder many domestic responsibilities.) Many fought vehemently against the sexual double-standard, and espoused greater female control over reproduction. Some called for "voluntary motherhood" with sexual intercourse under women's control; others like Margaret Sanger and Emma Goldman argued for greater sexual indulgence and the use of contraceptive devices. (see Gordon, 1976) Running through all these analyses was the insight that in both the public sphere and in domestic life sex created a division which made women of all races and economic classes, in very palpable ways, a subordinate group. The analysis of the multifaceted nature of women's inequality was one of the enduring contributions of the nineteenth-century feminists.

DOCUMENT 5

Jane Addams, "The Modern City and the Municipal Franchise for Women," NAWSA Convention, Baltimore, Maryland, February 7–13, 1906

It has been well said that the modern city is a stronghold of industrialism quite as the feudal city was a stronghold of militarism, but the modern cities fear no enemies and

Source: Buhle, Mari Jo and Paul, eds., *The Concise History of Women Suffrage* (Urbana: University of Illinois Press, 1978), p. 371.

rivals from without and their problems of government are solely internal. Affairs for the most part are going badly in these great new centres, in which the quickly-congregated population has not yet learned to arrange its affairs satisfactorily. Unsanitary housing, poisonous sewage, contaminated water, infant mortality, the spread of contagion, adulterated food, impure milk, smoke-laden air, ill-ventilated factories, dangerous occupations, juvenile crime, unwholesome crowding, prostitution and drunkenness are the enemies which the modern cities must face and overcome, would they survive. Logically their electorate should be made up of those who can bear a valiant part in this arduous contest, those who in the past have at least attempted to care for children, to clear houses, to prepare foods, to isolate the family from moral dangers; those who have traditionally taken care of that side of life which inevitably becomes the subject of municipal consideration and control as soon as the population is congested. To test the elector's fitness to deal with this situation by his ability to bear arms is absurd. These problems must be solved, if they are solved at all, not from the military point of view, not even from the industrial point of view, but from a third, which is rapidly developing in all the great cities of the world—the human-welfare point of view. . . .

City housekeeping has failed partly because women, the traditional housekeepers, have not been consulted as to its multiform activities. The men have been carelessly indifferent to much of this civic housekeeping, as they have always been indifferent to the details of the household. . . . The very multifariousness and complexity of a city government demand the help of minds accustomed to detail and variety of work, to a sense of obligation for the health and welfare of young children and to a responsibility for the cleanliness and comfort of other people. Because all these things have traditionally been in the hands of women, if they take no part in them now they are not only missing the education which the natural participation in civic life would bring to them but they are losing what they have always had.

DOCUMENT 6

Jane Addams, "Respect for the Law," The Independent, January 3, 1901

[M]any of the most atrocious public acts recorded in history have been committed by men who had convinced themselves that they were doing right. They either proceeded upon a false theory of conduct, or—what is much worse—they later invented a theory of conduct to cover and support their deeds.

One of these time-honored false theories has been that criminality can be suppressed and terrorized by exhibitions of brutal punishment; that crime can be prevented by cruelty.

Let us then assume that the Southern citizens who take part in and abet the lynching of negroes honestly believe that that is the only successful method of dealing with a certain class of crime [i.e. rape]; that they have become convinced that the Southern negro in his present undeveloped state must be frightened and subdued by terror; that, acting upon this theory, they give each lynching full

Source: Reprinted in *Lynching and Rape: An Exchange of Views*, ed., Bettina Aptheker (New York: The American Institute for Marxist Studies, 1977).

publicity and often gather together numerous spectators. We know that at least on one occasion excursion trains carried thousands of people to view a carefully planned lynching, in order that as many people as possible might be thoroughly frightened by the spectacle, and terrorized from committing the same crime. On this same assumption the living victim is sometimes horribly mutilated and his body later exhibited.

Let us give the Southern citizens the full benefit of this position, and assume that they have set aside trial by jury and all processes of law because they have become convinced that this brutal method of theirs is the most efficient method in dealing with a peculiar class of crime committed by one race against another. . . .

We would send this message to our fellow citizens of the South who are once more trying to suppress vice by violence: That the bestial in man, that which leads him to pillage and rape, can never be controlled by public cruelty and dramatic punishment, which too often cover fury and revenge. That violence is the most ineffectual method of dealing with crime, the most preposterous attempt to inculcate lessons of self control. A community has a right to protect itself from the criminal, to restrain him, to segregate him from the rest of society. But when it attempts revenge, when it persuades itself that exhibitions of cruelty result in reform it shows itself ignorant of all the teachings of history; it allows itself to be thrown back into the savage state of dealing with criminality.

It further runs a certain risk of brutalizing each spectator, of shaking his belief in law and order, of sowing seeds for future violence. It is certainly doubtful whether these scenes could be enacted over and over again, save in a community in which the hardening drama of slavery had once been seen, in which the devastation of war had taken place; and we may be reasonably sure that the next generation of the South cannot escape the result of the lawlessness and violence which are now being indulged in.

Brutality begets brutality; and proceeding on the theory that the negro is undeveloped, and therefore must be treated in this primitive fashion, is to forget that the immature pay little attention to statements, but quickly imitate what they see. The under-developed are never helped by such methods as these, for they learn only by imitation. The child who is managed by a system of bullying and terrorizing is almost sure to be the vicious and stupid child.

[T]he woman who is protected by violence allows herself to be protected as the woman of the savage is, and she must still be regarded as the possession of man. As her lord and master is strong or weak, so is the protection which she receives; . . . if she takes brute force as her protection, she must also accept the status she held when brute force alone prevailed.

I have purposely treated this subject on the theory of its ablest defenders; I have said nothing of the innumerable chances of punishing the wrong man; of the many other results of lawless methods; I have avoided confusing the main issue.

DOCUMENT 7

Ida B. Wells Barnett, "Lynching and the Excuse for It,"
The Independent, May 16, 1901

It was eminently befitting that THE INDEPENDENT's first number in the new century should contain a strong protest against lynching. The deepest dyed infamy of the nineteenth century was that which, in its supreme contempt for law, defied all constitutional guaranties of citizenship, and during the last fifteen years of the century put to death two thousand men, women and children, by shooting, hanging and burning alive. Well would it have been if every preacher in every pulpit in the land had made so earnest a plea as that which came from Miss Addams's forceful pen.

Appreciating the helpful influences of such a dispassionate and logical argument as that made by the writer referred to, I earnestly desire to say nothing to lessen the force of the appeal. At the same time an unfortunate presumption used as a basis for her argument works so serious, tho doubtless unintentional, an injury to the memory of thousands of victims of mob law, that it is only fair to call attention to this phase of the writer's plea. It is unspeakably infamous to put thousands of people to death without a trial by jury; it adds to that infamy to charge that these victims were moral monsters, when in fact, four-fifths of them were not so accused even by the fiends who murdered them.

Almost at the beginning of her discussion, the distinguished writer says:

"Let us assume that the Southern citizens who take part in and abet the lynching of negroes honestly believe that that is the only successful method of dealing with a certain class of crime."

It is this assumption, this absolutely unwarrantable assumption, that vitiates every suggestion which it inspires Miss Addams to make. It is the same baseless assumption which influences ninety-nine out of every one hundred persons who discuss this question. Among many thousand editorial clippings I have received in the past five years, ninety-nine per cent discuss the question upon the presumption that lynchings are the desperate effort of the Southern people to protect their women from black monsters, and while the large majority condemn lynching, the condemnation is tempered with a plea for the lyncher—that human nature gives way under such awful provocation and that the mob, insane for the moment, must be pitied as well as condemned. It is strange that an intelligent, law-abiding and fair minded people should so persistently shut their eyes to the facts in the discussion of what the civilized world now concedes to be America's national crime.

For an example in point: For fifteen years past, on the first day of each year, the *Chicago Tribune* has given to the public a carefully compiled record of all the lynchings of the previous year. . . . If the Southern citizens lynch negroes because "that is the only successful method of dealing with a certain class of crimes" [i.e. rape], then that class of crimes should be shown unmistakably by this record. Now consider the record.

It would be supposed that the record would show that all, or nearly all, lynchings were caused by outrageous assaults upon women; certainly that this particular offense would outnumber all other causes for putting human beings to death without a trial by jury and the other safeguards of our Constitution and laws.

But the record makes no such disclosure. Instead, it

Source: Reprinted in *Lynching and Rape: An Exchange of Views*, ed., Bettina Aptheker (New York: The American Institute for Marxist Studies, 1977).

shows that five women have been lynched, put to death with unspeakable savagery, during the past five years. They certainly were not under the ban of the outlawing crime. It shows that men, not a few, but hundreds, have been lynched for misdemeanors, while others have suffered death for no offense known to the law, the causes assigned being "mistaken identity," "insult," "bad reputation," "unpopularity," "violating contract," "running quarantine," "giving evidence," "frightening child by shooting at rabbits," etc. Then, strangest of all, the record shows that the sum total of lynchings for these offenses— not crimes—and for the alleged offenses which are only misdemeanors, greatly exceeds the lynchings for the very crime universally declared to be the cause of lynching.

Instead of being the sole cause of lynching, the crime upon which lynchers build their defense furnishes the least victims for the mob. In 1896 less than thirty-nine per cent of the negroes lynched were charged with this crime; in 1897, less than eighteen per cent; in 1898, less than sixteen per cent, and in 1900, less than fifteen per cent were so charged.

No good result can come from any investigation which refuses to consider the facts. A conclusion that is based upon a presumption, instead of the best evidence, is unworthy of a moment's consideration. The Christian and moral forces of the nation should insist that misrepresentation should have no place in the discussion of this all important question, that the figures of the lynching record should be allowed to plead, trumpet tongued, in defense of the slandered dead, that the silence of concession be broken and that truth, swift-winged and courageous, summon this nation to do its duty to exalt justice and preserve inviolate the sacredness of human life.

DOCUMENT 8

Muller v. Oregon (1908) 208 U.S. 412

Mr. Justice Brewer wrote for the Court.

The single question is the constitutionality of the statute under which the defendant was convicted, so far as it affects the work of a female in a laundry [by limiting the number of hours she can work]. . . .

We held in *Lochner v. New York*, 198 U.S. 45, that a law providing that no laborer shall be required or permitted to work in bakeries more than sixty hours in a week or ten hours in a day was not, as to men, a legitimate exercise of the police power of the state, but an unreasonable, unnecessary, and arbitrary interference with the right and liberty of the individual to contract in relation to his labor, and as such was in conflict with and void under [the Fourteenth Amendment of] the Federal Constitution. That decision is invoked by plaintiff in error as decisive of the question before us. But this assumes that the difference between the sexes does not justify a different rule respecting a restriction of the hours of labor.

That woman's physical structure and the performance of maternal functions place her at a disadvantage in the struggle for subsistence is obvious. This is especially true when the burdens of motherhood are upon her. Even when they are not, by abundant testimony of the medical fraternity continuance for a long time on her feet at work, repeating this from day to day, tends to injurious effects upon the body, and, as healthy mothers are essential to

Source: *Muller* v. *Oregon* (1908) 208 U.S. 412

vigorous offspring, the physical well-being of woman becomes an object of public interest and care in order to preserve the strength and vigor of the race.

Still again, history discloses the fact that woman has always been dependent upon man. He established his control at the outset by superior physical strength, and this control in various forms, with diminishing intensity, has continued to the present. As minors, though not to the same extent, she has been looked upon in the courts as needing especial care that her rights may be preserved. Education was long denied her, and while now the doors of the schoolroom are opened and her opportunities for acquiring knowledge are great, yet even with that and the consequent increase of capacity for business affairs it is still true that in the struggle for subsistence she is not an equal competitor with her brother. Though limitations upon personal and contractual rights may be removed by legislation, there is that in her disposition and habits of life which will operate against a full assertion of those rights. She will still be where some legislation to protect her seems necessary to secure a real equality of right. Doubtless there are individual exceptions, and there are many respects in which she has an advantage over him; but looking at it from the viewpoint of the effort to maintain an independent position in life, she is not upon an equality. Differentiated by these matters from the other sex, she is properly placed in a class by herself, and legislation designed for her protection may be sustained, even when like legislation is not necessary for men, and could not be sustained. It is impossible to close one's eyes to the fact that she still looks to her brother and depends upon him. Even though all restrictions on political, personal, and contractual rights were taken away, and she stood, so far as statutes are concerned, upon an absolutely equal plane with him, it would still be true that she is so constituted that she will rest upon and look to him for protection: that her physical structure and a proper discharge of her maternal functions—having in view not merely her own health, but the well-being of the race—justify legislation to protect her from the greed as well as the passion of man. The limitations which this statute places upon her contractual powers, upon her right to agree with her employer as to the time she shall labor, are not imposed soley for her benefit, but also largely for the benefit of all. Many words cannot make this plainer. The two sexes differ in structure of body, in the functions to be performed by each, in the amount of physical strength, in the capacity for long-continued labor, particularly when done standing, the influence of vigorous health upon the future well-being of the race, the self-reliance which enables one to assert full rights, and in the capacity to maintain the struggle for subsistence. This difference justifies a difference in legislation, and upholds that which is designed to compensate for some of the burdens which rest upon her.

We have not referred in this discussion to the denial of the elective franchise in the state of Oregon, for while that may disclose a lack of political equality in all things with her brother, that is not of itself decisive. The reason runs deeper, and rests in the inherent difference between the two sexes, and in the different functions in life which they perform.

For these reasons, and without questioning in any respect the decision in *Lochner v. New York*, we are of the opinion that it cannot be adjudged that the act in question is in conflict with the Federal Constitution, so far as it respects the work of a female in a laundry, and the judgment of the Supreme Court of Oregon is *Affirmed*.

"The Hearing on the Kirkland-Jenks Bill," Equal Rights, Vol. XVI, no. 6 (March 15, 1930)

Once again the question of whether or not women restaurant workers are to be exempted from the provisions of the law forbidding them to work between 10 P.M. and 6 A.M. was thrashed out in the State Capitol of New York when those who were for and those who were against the Kirkland-Jenks bill, which would exempt women restaurant workers from the provisions of the no-night-work law appeared at a hearing on February 26, called by the committees of labor and industries of the Senate and Assembly to present their arguments. The Kirkland-Jenks bill is sponsored by the Industrial Council of the National Women's Party.

The opposition was first heard. Mr. O'Hanlon, of the State Federation of Labor, appeared in opposition to the bill on the ground that it was an attempt to break down existing labor laws which, he said, had worked well and protected women from exhaustive hours of labor.

Lillian Moore, who claimed to be a waitress and to represent 3,000 waitresses in New York City, said: "We do not want night work. We have waitresses performing duties every day who will tell you the same thing. Fifty per cent of our membership are mothers. We are forced to leave our children in nurseries or with friends and at night the nurseries are not open. There are not many friends who will take care of our children in the evenings. The rest of our membership are young girls who will not work at night. They do not want to be insulted by men out at night who would not be out during the daytime." Five other women, who claimed that they represented waitresses' unions in Buffalo and elsewhere, appeared in opposition to the bill.

Mrs. Florence Kelley, of the Consumers' League, stated that the Consumers' League had to do with the original passing of the law prohibiting women from night work and said: "I want to call to your attention the fact that the tuberculosis death rate among young women has been increasing in spite of the efforts for the past six years to keep the right turn. The Children's Bureau has again printed the fact that every year in this country about 26,000 mothers of families die either in childbirth or because of diseases connected with childbirth. We pile up every year 26,000 motherless families in this country. We have, since 1920, accumulated a quarter of a million deaths of mothers. If women were as strong as men are, that record would not have been made."

Rose Schneiderman, president of the Woman's Trade Union League, . . . said: "I am sure that whatever arguments we are going to make, they will be the same arguments we have made for five, six or seven years. We are absolutely at one on the question of not touching the waitress law. We want the law to remain as it is today. Since we have not had night work, we have had a better social and moral life for the working girl.

ANNA HARBOTTLE WHITTLE, State Chairman of the National Woman's Party, before introducing the speakers in favor of the bill, asked Mr. Edmund B. Jenks, its introducer in the Assembly, to speak.

Mr. Jenks said: "I am proud to say that I was instrumental in putting through the Sheppard-Towner Maternity Bill. I have a friendly feeling for mothers. I had a mother who worked. I do not know that it did her very much harm. She worked on a farm, had ten kids and worked far into the night to keep things going. She died at 72. I do not know how long she might have lived if she had not worked. I am one of the people who believe that we cannot afford to curtail the right of individuals to sell their labor without some very substantial basis. Letting honest, self-respecting women work at night only restores to them the right they had before we curtailed their hours of employment. I believe every woman knows best where and when to labor and is just as capable to sell her labor as anyone here. If it is not safe for working girls to go home late at night we need remedial bills for that condition. If cities need mopping up, let us mop them up, but on their account not place restriction on the hours for a woman to work. I have no reason to doubt the statistics given on child death rate and the death rate following child-birth, but they have nothing to do with this bill. Women have the ballot and the same means of protecting themselves as men. My contribution to women lies in giving them a chance to say what hours in the 24 they shall work in restaurants."

Mrs. Whittle then introduced Frances G. Roberts, treasurer of the Industrial Council of the National Woman's Party, who said: ". . . Mr. Koveleski has said that one chief reason why he does not want this bill passed is that it would throw men out of work. Why should we not have an equal chance with men? As far as our health goes, I say we can fight tuberculosis better if we have proper food and homes. As for women dying in child-birth, I guess women always will do so, a certain percentage at least. It has never been proved that hard work made a woman die when giving birth to a child. A certain amount of protective legislation may be necessary, provided it applies to both sexes. There are instances in which an employer needs to be put into line and made to see the light. Make such laws. The adult woman, however, objects to being classed with children.

"Mr. Jenks spoke of the fact that in smaller cities the girls are not protected going home. There are certain occupations in which it is considered safe for girls to go home late at night. Telephone operators are pretty and attractive young women and we suppose that the police can adequately protect them. Scrub women, and trained nurses are abroad in the late night hours. It seems perfectly safe for girls who work in theatres to go home late. The jobs that men do not want they don't get so chivalrous about. (Applause.)

"When they don't want the jobs, the men leave us alone to work out our own plans. They immediately begin to worry about our health and welfare when they can use the jobs themselves. Take the history of women who have been forced out of jobs. Women used to work on street cars as conductors. One girl who was thrown out because of so-called 'protective' laws told me she had never been able since to get so good a job. She made over $5.00 a day on the street cars. She earns now about $15.00 a week and has harder hours than she had on the cars. It is decidedly unfair that a law should be given us which allows us no decision as to the time, place and hours we shall work. We ask for an equal chance with men to earn our living. Our food costs just as much as men's. We want the chance to choose our own hours of labor. I have had to teach men and break them into the jobs they have taken since women have been precluded from the late watch. It went against the grain to do it." . . .

Beatrice Stevenson, of the King's County Republican Committee and New York State Nursing Association, was then introduced and said: "I have listened to the waitresses who have spoken against this bill today. It seemed to me that they believe this bill would compel them to work at night. Those women who do not want to work at night are under no compulsion to do so. . . . I happen to be a member of one of the healthiest professions—that of nursing. I recognize the rights of a country to protect its workers. However, if laws are necessary, they should be made for both men and women. They should be based upon the nature of the work and not upon the sex of the worker. In the name of justice and reason I ask you to further the passage of this bill."

Mr. EVANS, counsel for the National Restaurant Association, stated that the proposed bill, which was not their bill, would merely permit restaurants to employ women workers over the age of 21 after 10 o'clock at night and before 6 o'clock in the morning. From the standpoint of the restaurants, he said, the existing law seemed ridiculous. A man engaged in operating a respectable restaurant now cannot have a woman to wash his dishes after 10 o'clock at night. He can't have a woman come in to scrub his floors before 6 in the morning. "Can you point out to me, gentlemen of this committee or the opponents of the bill, where there is any more danger in a woman working in a restaurant after 10 o'clock than in a dining room or kitchen of a hotel, where they are allowed to work?"

Mr. Fred Seames, of the Buffalo Restaurant Association, said that the present law was unfair to the restaurant industry, the third largest in the country.

Senator Kirkland, who was unable to be present, asked to be recorded as being unalterably in favor of the amendment.

by Mary A. Murray,
Chairman of the Industrial Council
National Woman's Party

Chapter 4

Was there a "New Deal" for Women?

Recent work by historians of women has revised the traditional view of the 1930s as a rather bleak decade for feminism, a time when women's issues were forced to take a back seat to the pressing concerns of the Great Depression. More women served in government office during the 1930s than in any previous decade, indeed in any decade until the 1960s. Women also moved into the Democratic Party organization in significant numbers, and took an active role in the Communist Party, home of many social activists and idealists in the 1930s. In addition, women had a major influence on much New Deal legislation. Those women who worked for general social change bent their efforts to make sure that women and their needs were not forgotten. Despite the very different political and economic contexts which confronted them, there were clear ideological and sociological links between the feminist activists of the first two decades of the century and those of the 1930s. Those links formed part of the deep and continuous feminist tradition in American politics.

A. Women as Officeholders

Franklin Delano Roosevelt, first elected President in 1932, appointed women to federal offices in unprecedented numbers. Women had held such offices before: Julia Lathrop was head of the Children's Bureau when it was established in 1912; Mary Anderson was appointed to direct the Women's Bureau of the Department of Labor in 1920; Helen Hamilton Gardener and Jessie Dell served on the Civil Service Commission. But, as Molly Dewson, one of Roosevelt's political allies remarked, "Twelve appointments by five Presidents in 24 years was not an exhilarating record." The list of Roosevelt's appointees included Frances Perkins, Secretary of Labor; Ellen Sullivan Woodward, head of Women's and Professional Projects in the Works Progress Administration (WPA); Josephine Roche, Assistant Secretary of the Treasury; Nellie Taylor Ross, Director of the Mint; Mary McLeod Bethune, Office of Minority Affairs of the National Youth Administration; and Florence Allen, U.S. Court of Appeals. (Ware, 1982, 89–90)

Several factors contributed to the movement of women into public office. Those developing the social programs of the New Deal drew heavily on the experiences of organizations like the National Consumers' League (NCL), the Women's Trade Union League (WTUL), and the various settlement houses. Women's experience in the development and delivery of social services gave them valuable expertise which the government needed. In addition, the proliferation of government programs meant that many new jobs were being created, often outside of entrenched bureaucracies, and this facilitated women's appointments. Eleanor Roosevelt and Frances Perkins lobbied strenuously for the appointment of women they knew to be capable, and Franklin Roosevelt was receptive to their suggestions. The women who moved into government positions by-and-large came out of social service, trade union, and educational organizations. They shared a firm commitment both to social reform and to increasing women's role in politics and government. As Susan Ware has shown, a women's network developed among many New Deal female administrators, further encouraging women's entry into government office. (Ware, 1981, ch. 1) At the center of this network was Eleanor Roosevelt. Her friendship with many New Deal administrators advanced both women's programs and their political careers.

The women's network which Ware has described was made up exclusively of white women, despite the fact that one of the most important women in the New Deal was Mary McLeod Bethune (1875–1955), who headed the Office of Minority Affairs in the National Youth Administration (NYA). Bethune, who was born in 1875, was the fifteenth of seventeen children born to parents who had been slaves. She attended Scotia Seminary in North Carolina, and in 1894 entered what later became the Moody Bible Institute in Chicago, hoping to become a missionary. Thwarted by the fact that there were no available posts for black Presbyterian missionaries in Africa when she graduated, Bethune became a teacher, and later a civil leader in Daytona, Florida. In 1929 she expanded her school and founded Bethune-Cookman College in Jacksonville. Bethune rose to national prominence through club work in the National Association of Colored Women, of which she was elected president in 1924. In 1935 Bethune founded the National Council of Negro Women, a coalition of black women's associations, and served as its president until 1949. In 1927, when Franklin Roosevelt was Governor of New York, Bethune met Eleanor Roosevelt at a reception, and in time the two became political allies and good friends. Bethune educated Eleanor Roosevelt on many problems of black Americans, and Roosevelt in turn used her influence to secure Bethune's appointment to the NYA. Bethune guided the NYA toward hiring more black administrators at the state and regional levels, broadening black participation in the school aid program, and increasing employment opportunities for black youth. Not very successful at the last task during the Depression, her efforts bore fruit during World War II when some defense industries which had never before hired blacks did so. Bethune also helped organize the Federal Council on Negro Affairs, popularly known as Franklin Roosevelt's "black cabinet," which pushed for relief programs for blacks and for nondiscrimination in government facilities and employment. The fact that Bethune was not part of the "women's network" in Washington, despite her office and her personal friendship with Eleanor Roosevelt, is a comment on the pervasive power of social segregation and on the attitudes which women brought to their jobs in Washington which often made inter-racial sisterhood an elusive goal. (Ware, 1982, 102)

B. Women in the Democratic Party Organization

At the 1919 Convention of the National American Women's Suffrage Association, when suffrage was all but within reach, Carrie Chapman Catt had admonished the delegates that

> The next battle is going to be inside the parties, and we are not going to stay outside and let all the reactionaries have their way on the inside! Within every party there is a struggle between progressive and reactionary elements. Candidates are a compromise between these extremes. You will be disillusioned, you will find yourselves in a political penumbra where most of the men are. They will be glad to see you, you will be flattered. But if you stay long enough, you will discover a little denser thing which is the umbra of the political party—the people who are picking the candidates, doing the real work that you and the men sanction at the polls. You won't be welcome, but there is the place to go. You will see the real thing in the center with the door locked tight. You will have a long hard fight before you get inside . . . but you must move right up to the center. (Peck, 1944, 325)

Women's movement into such party councils was slow, and is not yet fully achieved. The first dramatic change in women's rather peripheral roles in Democratic and Republican party councils came in 1933, when Molly Dewson was appointed as the first full-time director of the Women's Division of the Democratic National Committee. She took a particular interest in recruiting undecided or independent voters to the Democratic Party, leaving the relations with ward bosses and solid Democratic voters to James Farley, head of the Democratic National Committee. She developed a highly successful Reporter Plan, which created networks of women in Democratic County organizations. These women studied the new policies of federal agencies and "reported" and explained them in their communities. The Reporter system both recruited women and disseminated information about New Deal programs. By the time of the 1936 campaign, Dewson had 15,000 active and informed Reporters able to speak for the Democratic Party. The Women's Division also took over publication of the *Democratic Digest* in 1935, and increased its circulation from 1,600 to 26,000 by 1938. During the 1936 campaign the Women's Division popularized the highly effective Rainbow Fliers, each flier containing information about a specific field of governmental activity such as labor, finance, agriculture, or business. (Ware, 1981, 68–81)

Dewson was above all a loyal Democrat, but she brilliantly combined her interest in strengthening the party with efforts to increase women's participation in politics. Her efforts tapped women's energies at all levels of the party organization, from county committees to appointive offices in the federal government. The political skills women developed in the 1930s were critical to their struggles for greater rights and increased political participation in future years.

C. Women in the Communist Party

Many women who brought feminist concerns to their work were active in the Communist Party in the 1930s, the decade of that party's greatest influence in the United States. It has been estimated that of 10,000 CP members in 1933, sixteen percent were women, equally divided between housewives and workers. Of these women, 300 were black. By the end of the decade, between thirty and forty percent of the CP were women. Women's position within the CP was fraught with paradox. Susan Ware has argued that "few other groups in American society held more enlightened views about women's roles in the 1930s, and many held considerably worse. The Communist Party was one of the few to encourage public discussion of women's issues during this decade." (Ware, 1982, 124) Several women rose to considerable prominence in the CP. Anna Damon and Margaret Cowl headed the CP's Women's Commission; Elizabeth Gurley Flynn joined the CP in 1936 and was elected to its national committee in 1938; Anita Whitney was elected chairperson of the California party organization in 1936; Ella Reeve ("Mother") Bloor, a women's suffragist and strike organizer, served on the central committee throughout the 1930s. The CP also opposed racism, and when Mother Bloor organized a U.S. delegation to attend an International Women's Conference in Paris in 1934, four of the delegates were black. (Davis, 1981, 156) Rank-and-file women, did not, however, inevitably fare well in the CP, particularly, it seemed, wives of organizers. These women were expected to perform all the domestic work in addition to helping with political activities, and were often asked to subordinate all other interests to their husbands' work.

This paradox between a serious commitment to the eradication of oppression of all kinds and a blindness to certain forms of subjection in women's daily lives stemmed from the fact that the CP believed in the primary importance of the class-struggle. The liberation of working-class women, it held, would come about simultaneously with that of working-class men. Mary Inman, in her book, *In Woman's Defense*, showed how overcoming sex oppression would require more attention than Marxist theorists and most male CP activists had yet paid it. [Document 10] Her book met with a chilly reception from those male leaders who refused to acknowledge the possibility of divergent interests between working-class husbands and wives. Women in leftist organizations in the 1960s would experience some of the same kinds of frustrations with male colleagues who refused to take seriously feminists' analyses of the multifaceted nature of women's oppression.

D. Women and Legislation

The women recruited to government under Franklin Roosevelt made significant contributions to formulating as well as to implementing New Deal legislation. Many of them had extensive experience in organizations like the NCL and the WTUL, whose goals were reflected in legislation like the National Industrial Recovery Act (NIRA) which (among other provisions) contained stipulations for minimum wages and maximum hours, prohibited child labor, and provided for consumer representation. Drafting of the Social Security Act of 1935 was due in great part to the efforts of Frances Perkins, Secretary of Labor, and Arthur Altmeyer of the Children's Bureau. Perkins and Altmeyer drew on the research and proposals generated over twenty years by the NCL, the American Association for Labor Legislation, and the American Association for Old Age Security. In similar fashion Perkins drew on the past experiences of social feminist organizations when drafting the legislation which became the Fair Labor Standards Act of 1938, particularly those sections dealing with maximum hours, minimum wages, and child labor. Ellen Sullivan Woodward, head of the Women's and Professional Projects for the WPA, took particular interest in and responsibility for programs for women, particularly jobs and job training, and the short-lived resident camps for unemployed women.

Valuable as this New Deal legislation was, much of it scarcely touched black women. In 1930, according to Women's Bureau statistics, ninety percent of black women workers were domestics or farm laborers, occupations which were not covered by the NIRA codes, the Fair Labor Standards Act, or the Social Security Act. Black women were also far less likely to be provided relief under such federally funded but locally administered programs as the Public Works Administration (PWA) and the Works Progress Administration (WPA). For some this led to local organizing and collective efforts among black women. One North Carolina woman wrote to Harry Hopkins, head of the WPA, "Mr. Hopkins, colored women have been turned out of different jobs projects to make us take other jobs we mentioned and white women were hired & sent for & given places that colored women was made to leave or quit. . . . We the Workers Council . . . wish you to tell us why." (Baxandall, Gordon, and Reverby, 1976, 251) The National Youth Administration, where the influence of Mary McLeod Bethune was strong, had a relatively good record in fending off discrimination, and lobbied for the needs of black women, but many New Deal agencies overlooked the discrimination and segregation in their programs which exacerbated the economic plight of blacks.

Feminists were concerned with legislation which dealt particularly with women, as well as with general economic and social reform. Section 213 of the 1932 National Economy Act (NEA), which stipulated that a husband and wife could not both work for the federal government at the same time, raised their ire. Despite Roosevelt's general support for women and women's issues, he did not oppose this ban on nepotism. The entire NEA was repealed in 1937, but by then Section 213 had forced many married women out of government service. (Ware, 1981, 77–79)

In 1936 women in public life, particularly Mary Anderson of the Women's Bureau and social researcher Mary Van Kleek tried to unify women in the face of the rise of "reactionary forces everywhere" by drafting and circulating a "Woman's Charter." [Document 11] The Charter called for full political rights, education, job opportunity, guarantees against physically harmful conditions of employment and economic exploitation, and compensation without discrimination due to sex. The last paragraph of the Woman's Charter declared that "Where special exploitation of women workers exists, . . . such conditions shall be corrected through social and labor legislation, which the world's experience shows to be necessary." As Mary Anderson remarked in her memoirs, the movement to have all the major women's organizations adopt the Women's Charter was "a complete flop." The National Women's Party would have nothing to do with it because of the clause about special legislation for women. The YWCA, the General Federation of Women's Clubs, the League of Women Voters, the National Council of Catholic Women, and the WTUL, all of whom had helped draft the Charter, had to seek endorsement from their membership. This time-consuming process sapped the vitality of the Charter movement. Although it died aborning, the Women's Charter was nonetheless an interesting reflection of feminist concerns in the later 1930s. Nor was it altogether ineffective. It served as the basis for a resolution adopted by the International Labor Organization in June, 1937, requesting members to further the goals of sex equality in employment. It also inspired women like Mary Anderson to press for the section of the United Nations Charter which states that "The United Nations shall place no restrictions on the eligibility of men and women to participate in any capacity and under conditions of equality in its principal and subsidiary organs." (Anderson, 1951, 210–214) The effort to insure that women were placed in a situation of equality in this new international body was an outgrowth of the determined efforts of the women of the 1930s to move increasing numbers of women into positions of authority and public responsibility. The women who helped draft the United Nations Charter acted in the well-established tradition of activism on behalf of women which stretched back through the New Deal to the social feminists and suffragists of the early years of the twentieth century.

DOCUMENT 10

Mary Inman, In Woman's Defense
Ch. 27: "The Housewife's Role in Social Production"

Workers of no other group have had their importance so ignored and denied as present day housewives.

Because productive tasks once performed in the home are now performed elsewhere, the housewife's work now is under-rated to such an extent that she is considered in certain quarters to even be living in ease and parasitism.

Adding to this erroneous notion, and appearing to support it, is the fact that the 22 million housewives who work only at home and do all their work have no earnings or income of their own and must depend upon their food, clothing and housing being bought with money earned by their husbands.

Now this support a husband gives his wife comes out of production, and if she is not useful, in fact indispensable

Source: Mary Inman, *In Woman's Defense* (Los Angeles, 1940), 141–145, 151–155.

to the owners of industry, why do they permit 22 million women to subsist on the proceeds of industry?

There can be only one answer. Under certain conditions it profits them. Under certain conditions it is irreplaceable.

Let us illustrate the point further: The work of a cook in a logging camp is a necessary part of the production of lumber. The services of all the cooks in all the camps, restaurants and eating places wherever productive workers are fed, are a necessary part of production. And for the same reason, the work of the cooks in the homes of productive workers is also, at present, a necessary part of production.

The labor of a woman, who cooks for her husband, who is making tires in the Firestone plant in Southgate, California, is essentially as much a part of the production of automobile tires as the cooks and waitresses in the cafes where Firestone workers eat.

And all the wives of all the Firestone workers, by the necessary social labor they perform in the home, have a part in the production of Firestone Tires, and their labor is as inseparably knit into those tires as is the labor of their husbands.

And in the same way, the labor of housewives in the homes of productive workers who perform the services of keeping clothing washed and beds and floors clean, is also an indispensable part of production.

The middle class housewife then, who did useful housework for a husband engaged in such work of production and distribution, or for sons so engaged, or for sons who were already, or preparing to become, technicians, engineers or teachers for the capitalists, or for daughters who would become the working wives of men so employed, such middle class housewives filled a socially useful role in their day to day work, and they contributed to the cumulative building of the great factory process that is modern America.

Housewives of both the middle and working classes helped create this wealth that is America today, and part of it belongs to them by right of toil.

Ch. 29: Outmoded Housework

A great deal of sentimental nonsense has been written about the work housewives do, tending to prove they can never escape it. Yet, if we trace down each of these sentimental idealizations, we find that it is definitely tied to poverty and disappears where persons have the means to lead a life in keeping with what the entire family desires and considers to be a high standard of living.

A great deal of the work formerly done in the home is now done socially even under capitalism, but the results are mainly appropriated by individual owners. Weaving and the making of clothing, the making of beddings and canning of foodstuffs have become profitable sources of income for factory owners.

The new method is more efficient and more scientific. Persons specially trained to do these tasks, work with others so trained, and they work regular hours and then are free.

The great lags in this progressive trend have been in the production of cooked foods, in the nursing and care of children, and in household cleaning and tidying. Laundering has lagged amazingly. This despite the fact that it is one service that could be done effectively with machinery at central points.

In a city of 500,000 people, containing, say, 100,000 working and lower middle class homes, 100,000 women are planning how to get the windows washed, the curtains cleaned, the clothing washed and ironed and the shopping done.

On 100,000 fires, skillets are smoking and pots boiling as 100,000 cooks cook 100,000 meals in our typical city of 500,000 persons. If there is an equal number of coffee and tea drinkers, 50,000 coffee pots will boil and 50,000 tea pots will steep.

Household hours average at least 50 hours a week, and on farms where there are babies they average 75, according to U. S. Labor Bulletin No. 155.

Now there are in the United States not 100,000 but 26 million households, where a minimum of 26 million persons, either in the capacity of servants or housewives, expend some 200 million hours of labor every day.

If we take into account that this work could probably be done in one-tenth the time, or less, by 3 million of these women, the enormity of this social waste becomes apparent.

If women in 26 million households are ever to escape the present out of date method of performing household work, their work must be reorganized so that it can be done more efficiently.

The feudalistic system that binds the Negro people in the United States has a territorial foundation in the plantation Black Belt in the South. The feudalistic system of women's work is not founded on land boundaries, but extends over all the nation and exists in industrial centers, where isolated home units, in which women toil at hand labor, stand side by side with factories where production is mechanized and specialized.

It is also fallacious to assume, as some socialists do, that nothing can be done under capitalism to improve housewives' outmoded method of work, and that we must first have socialism before women put their minds to this problem and tackle its solution.

This attitude is as illogical as saying that workers must wait for socialism to obtain higher wages, and have the conditions of their work improved, or that old persons must wait for pensions, or the unemployed sick for social medical care.

DOCUMENT 11

"The Women's Charter," 1936

This Charter is a general statement of the social and economic objectives of women, for women and for society as a whole, insofar as these can be embodied in legislation and governmental administration. It is put forward in order that there may be an agreed formulation of the purposes to which a large number of women's organizations throughout the world already are committed. It is recognized that some of the present specific needs which it seeks to remedy should disappear as society develops the assurance of a more complete life for every person; and some of its objectives would establish conditions which should be attainable for all persons, so that in promoting them for women it is hoped thereby to bring nearer the time of their establishment for all.

Source: Mary Anderson, *Woman at Work* (Minneapolis: University of Minnesota, 1951), 211–212.

Women shall have full political and civil rights; full opportunity for education; full opportunity for work according to their individual abilities, with safeguards against physically harmful conditions of employment and economic exploitation; they shall receive compensation, without discrimination because of sex. They shall be assured security of livelihood, including the safeguarding of motherhood. The provisions necessary for the establishment of these standards, shall be guaranteed by government, which shall insure also the right of united action toward the attainment of these aims.

Where special exploitation of women workers exists, such as low wages which provide less than the living standards attainable, unhealthful working conditions, or long hours of work which result in physical exhaustion and denial of the right to leisure, such conditions shall be corrected through social and labor legislation, which the world's experience shows to be necessary.

Chapter 5

World War II and the Post-War Decade: Women in the 1940s and 1950s

As the Great Depression shaped the lives of virtually all women in the 1930s, so World War II and its effects dominated Americans' experiences in the 1940s and the early 1950s. The war drew women into the public realm, both out of the desire to contribute to the national effort and from economic necessity. The resultant changes in many women's lives were dramatic. Some entered the military, the first time American women had been recruited into the armed forces. Many more went to the front as nurses. Others entered the labor force in unprecedented numbers, and many of these took jobs in heavy industries which had previously closed their doors to women. Virtually all women participated in the war effort through the purchase of war bonds, rationing, sewing or knitting for the troops, victory gardening or volunteer work. Despite these changes in everyday life, however, many traditional attitudes and values survived the war intact. (The most dramatic disruption of women's lives, of course, occurred among the Japanese Americans moved to detention camps. Their experiences are beyond the scope of this short chapter.) Having weathered the military crisis, many Americans sought to hold onto their wartime gains and to return to "normalcy" and stability. As Susan Hartmann has commented the "continuing attachment to the prewar social order and values was nowhere more apparent than in the area of sex roles and women's status." (Hartmann, 1982, 12) This disjuncture between women's activities during the war years and deeply-rooted social beliefs about women's place would continue in the postwar decade.

A. Women and Military Service

The most dramatic challenge to women's traditional sex roles was the incorporation of women into the armed services. Indeed, one of the most persistent arguments against women's suffrage was that women should not have the vote since they were exempt from the ultimate obligation of citizenship, bearing arms for the nation. That argument carried considerable weight until World War I when women's efforts on the home front and as nurses and civilian support staff overseas bolstered the case for women's suffrage. Women had, of course, performed war-related jobs in every armed conflict since the Revolution, and the Navy had enlisted women as "yeoman (F)"

during World War I; in none of these conflicts, however, were women regular members of the armed services, as they were in World War II.

In March, 1942, the strictures against women in the military crumbled when Congress created the Women's Auxiliary Army Corps, which became simply the Women's Army Corps or WAC in 1943. Edith Nourse Rogers, congresswoman from Massachusetts, was the author of the bill creating the WAC. Rogers had seen American women at work at the front during World War I, and wanted not only to bolster America's military preparedness, but also to insure that whenever women served the military in the future they would be entitled to military status, protection, and benefits denied them after World War I. [Document 12] In July the Navy enlisted Women Accepted for Volunteer Emergency Service (WAVES) on the same basis as male reservists. By November the Coast Guard had created the SPARS (named from the Coast Guard motto, *Semper Paratus*), and the Marines accepted women by February of 1943. In all, about 350,000 women entered the military during the war. National policy forced the services to recruit black women, which they did reluctantly. More than 4000 black women, including 100 officers, served in segregated units in the WAC, although they never constituted more than six percent of the WAC. Black enlisted women were segregated in barracks, mess halls, and recreational facilities, and were sent to field assignments in all-black units. Opportunities for educated black women were greatly restricted in WAC units because segregationist policies did not allow them to be placed where they could best be utilized. The WAVES, Marines, and SPARS were all-white until late in the war. The Navy argued that since black men were eligible to enlist only for a few types of Navy positions, black Waves were not needed to replace them. President Roosevelt found such reasoning spurious, and insisted that all the armed services recruit black women. (Campbell, 1984, 20–25; Hartmann, 1984, 40–41)

The main impetus for recruiting women was to free male soldiers in clerical positions for combat. Despite the fact that there were 1,000,000 civilian clerks (mostly women) working for the War and Navy Departments by VE-Day, much military paperwork was handled by men in uniform; in 1944, thirty-five percent of the Army was assigned to clerical work. Women in uniform initially were assigned almost exclusively to typing and stenographic jobs, but as the war progressed more opportunities opened in manual and technical jobs. (Campbell, 1984, 31–32) Female officers had to be recruited from the civilian population and trained in military command in a matter of weeks. After the war only a few women chose to remain in uniform, but in 1948 President Truman signed the Armed Services Integration Act which created places for women in the regular services and the reserves. The military was never again an all-male preserve.

Although the leadership of the armed services had strongly advocated the recruitment of women, rank-and-file soldiers, few of whom ever came into direct contact with Wacs or Waves, expressed hostility to women in the military. In 1943 a rumor campaign which attacked women in uniform as being either lesbians or sexually promiscuous heterosexuals spread across the nation. It was so pernicious that the Pentagon, fearing Nazi involvement, asked the FBI to investigate. The FBI concluded that U.S. servicemen had started and sustained the rumors. Stories that Wacs and Waves were often drunk and were sexually loose even got transformed in some quarters to the belief that they were government-issue concubines. (Campbell, 1984, 39) One cause of the resentment was the government's original recruiting slogan (which was quickly dropped) that a woman could release a man for warfare, a prospect which understandably alienated some soldiers who faced the prospect of transfer from an office job to the front.

But the rumor campaign reflected that fact that women recruits posed much more subtle threats as well. Women in the military upset deeply rooted convictions about the proper relationship between men and women, and about women's appropriate roles in society. Women in uniform challenged the notion that men were supposed to protect women. Women's entry into the military, even in limited numbers and very limited positions, posed a fundamental challenge to the notion of separate spheres and men's and women's different natures and roles. Some men found this a threat to their self-understanding and their sense of masculinity alike.

B. Women and the Labor Force

The movement of women into the civilian labor force during World War II was less dramatic but numerically much more significant than women's entry into the armed services. Between 1940 and 1944 the number of employed women rose from 12,000,000 to 18,200,000. Many found employment in manufacturing and heavy industry plants which had previously not hired women. Steel, machinery, shipbuilding, aircraft and auto factories employed 230,000 women in 1939; in 1944, 2,690,000 women were employed in munitions, aircraft, shipbuilding, and related industries. Overall, between 1940 and 1946 the percentage of the labor force which was female increased by ten percent, from twenty-six percent to thirty-six percent. The composition of the female labor force itself changed as married women and older women took jobs. One out of every ten married women entered the labor force during the war, and by the war's end there were more married women than single women in the labor force, an unprecedented situation. More women with children also took jobs than ever before; the proportion of working mothers rose from 7.8 percent in 1940 to 12.1 percent in 1944. (Campbell, 1984, 72–73; Hartmann, 1982, 78)

Patterns of employment among black women did not change so dramatically, a reflection of the fact that a larger proportion of black women were already in the paid labor force at the start of the war. The proportion of black women wage-earners rose from thirty-three to forty percent, in absolute numbers from 1,500,000 to 2,100,000. Their share of the female labor force, however, fell from 13.8 percent to 12.5 percent, a result of a combination of factors: the influx of white women workers, the high pre-war employment of black women, and the greater employment opportunities of black men during the war. Black women's employment outside of domestic service did show a substantial increase, with black women moving into service positions (maids, cooks, cleaners) in hotels, restaurants and businesses, and into factory jobs. Also as a result of this movement, the proportion of black female population doing farm work fell by fifty percent during the war.

The federal government in theory supported equal employment opportunity, but black women faced both racial and sexual discrimination. When A. Philip Randolph, head of the Brotherhood of Sleeping Car Porters, proposed a march on Washington to protest the government's failure to insure black people's access to jobs and housing, President Roosevelt issued Executive Order 8802 banning discrimination in defense industries or the government on the basis of "race, creed, color, or national origin." The Fair Employment Practices Commission (FEPC) was established to protect the employment of minorities. Its only sanction, however, was withdrawal of war contracts from companies which violated its guidelines, a sanction it was reluctant to apply, since uninterrupted production was a top war-time priority. Numerous case studies documented the difficulties faced by black workers in general, and by black women in particular, as they sought to move from domestic and farm labor into manufacturing and factory work. Several of these studies testified to the importance of the NYA programs developed under Mary McLeod Bethune in promoting the industrial employment of blacks. [Document 13]

Government policies encouraged increased female labor force participation. Industrial productivity was a key component of the war effort. The Office of War Information (OWI) produced propaganda pictures portraying "Rosie the Riviter," acetylene torch in hand, doing her part to support the military effort overseas. The National War Labor Board (NWLB) tried to stimulate female employment by requiring equal pay for equal work in war-related industries. In 1943 the Lanham Act provided federal funds for child-care centers in an effort to curb absenteeism among mothers with young children and to recruit others.

These measures, however, were put forward with some ambivalence. Even as advertising campaigns urged women to take non-traditional jobs, they sought to assimilate those jobs to traditional women's work. Processes in munitions manufacture were compared to running a sewing machine or vacuum cleaner. "If you've used an electric mixer in your kitchen, you can learn to run a drill press. If you've followed recipes exactly in making cakes, you can learn to load a shell," read a billboard in 1943. (Baxandall, Gordon, and Reverby, 1976, 284) The NWLB's equal pay stipulations contained loopholes allowing women to be categorized differently than men doing essentially the same work. Federally sponsored day-care, for its part, met only a fraction of the need for such programs, and by 1946 federal funding had ended. The OWI, the War Manpower Council, and the War Advertising Council all encouraged women's entry into non-traditional employment, but always suggested that such jobs would be temporary, women's patriotic response to an exceptional situation.

When the war ended, the same kinds of forces which had drawn women into the labor force moved them out again. The number of employed women, which had risen from 12,000,000 to 18,000,000 between 1940 and 1944, fell back to 15,000,000 in 1947. The Women's Bureau, which foresaw the postwar cutbacks, conducted an extensive survey in 1944–45 of working women in ten manufacturing areas about their post-war plans. It revealed that seventy-five percent of these women wanted to continue to work after the war. Publicizing their findings was one way in which the Bureau sought to retain positions in the paid labor force, particularly in industry, for married and single women alike. [Document 14] They faced stiff odds, however. The number of women in steel, machinery, shipbuilding, aircraft, and auto factories plummeted. As the war drew to a close the OWI issued films celebrating the return of "normalcy." Many munitions and war production plants closed. Other industries cut back severely. As soldiers were demobilized, some women were more than happy to turn their jobs over to veterans and to return home. Others, however, were forced out of well-paying jobs they wished to keep, and black women who had just recently entered the industrial labor force were especially hard hit by the post-war loss of factory jobs for women. (Woloch, 1984, 468–69)

C. The Post-War Decade

Women's entry into the military and the civilian labor force did not come about as the result of a feminist campaign to move women into the public arena but in response to the extraordinary conditions of war. Indeed, at the same time that the exigencies of war moved women into new spheres of activity, feminist organizations were on the wane. Their decline had begun in the 1930s, even though the National Woman's Party, the League of Women Voters, and the Women's Trade Union League had valiantly joined forces to combat Section 213 of the National Economy Act which prohibited the employment of both husband and wife in the federal government, and to oppose discrimination against women in federal relief projects. Ironically, the greatest cooperative effort of many of the women's organizations in the 1940s was the formation of a coalition to defeat what they dubbed the "Unequal Rights Amendment." The Women's Bureau, the League of Women Voters, the American Association of University Women, the YWCA, the National Congresses of Catholic and Jewish Women, the New York branch of the WTUL, and twenty-five trade union groups all pitted themselves against the National Women's Party, the General Federation of Women's Clubs, and the National Women Lawyers' Association who favored the Equal Rights Amendment. In 1946 when the ERA reached the Senate, it failed to win the necessary two-thirds majority, a pattern repeated in 1950 and 1953.

The decline of broad-based feminist agitation was due in part to the ascendancy of other issues during the Depression and World War II which demanded the attention of politically active women. Older women also failed to recruit younger followers, and young women who had no experience of the suffrage struggle did not identify readily with "women's issues" as such. Nearly two decades of crisis, scarcity and sacrifices also spurred a desire

for "normalcy." Substantial numbers of women and men alike wanted what was regarded as the traditional family, headed by a male bread-winner and sustained and nurtured by a stay-at-home wife and mother. Popular psychology fed the notion that women who sought paid work or even extended activity outside the home were neurotic, ill-adjusted, and unable to accept their femininity.

At the same time, however, changes had been set in motion which would in time give rise to a resurgence of feminist ideology and activity. The absence of men during the war years had expanded women's experiences in the workplace, in civic organizations, in education, and in political life. Despite the rapid drop in women's employment right after World War II, that trend was reversed by 1947. By the end of the decade, thirty-one percent of adult women were in the labor force, many of them older and married women. Organizations like the League of Women Voters, the General Federation of Business and Professional Women, and the American Association of University Women continued to lobby for equal pay, greater access to job opportunities, and expanded political representation for women. The Women's Bureau reinforced these efforts by working for women's rights from within the government. The seeds of the black Civil Rights movement were also being sown in the post-war years, and that movement would nourish the renewed growth of feminism as well. The growth of suburbia, the baby-boom, and the social and political conservatism of the late 1940s and early 1950s masked the fact that the war years had altered in significant and irreversible ways woman's relationship to the public sphere.

DOCUMENT 12

Edith Nourse Rogers on the Women's Auxiliary Army Corps Act, U. S. House of Representatives, 1942.

Mr. ANDREWS. Mr. Chairman, I now yield 10 minutes to the gentlewoman from Massachusetts [Mrs. ROGERS], the author of the bill.

Mrs. ROGERS of Massachusetts. Mr. Chairman, almost a year ago I introduced this bill in Congress, on May 28, 1941, but the proposal for an organization of women to serve as noncombatants with the Army of the United States has long been in my mind. So far back as the first World War, when I was in England and France, I saw the need for such an adjunct to our military forces. Great Britain had a well-organized, smoothly operated women's auxiliary during the last war. I was thrown in close contact with them, worked with them myself, and came to appreciate and realize how extremely valuable the auxiliaries are in their performance of tasks for which women are suited or which they can do with equal facility as men. Even then I felt that our military forces should have an auxiliary force—one recognized as official, and one authorized by law to serve with the Army and to be subject to military control. In our first World War we did have women who served and who gave fine service. There were dietitians, physiotherapists, telephone operators—in fact, a number of categories—but their status was vague. Of course, nurses served as a part of our military services. They were not under military control in the strictest sense of the

Source: The Congressional Record, vol. 88 part 2 (March 17, 1942), 2582–84.

word. They received no compensation of any kind in the event they were sick or injured—and many were. It was a most unsatisfactory arrangement and has been the cause of much dissatisfaction ever since the Armistice. Many members of Congress have felt as I do, that these women who gave of their service, unselfishly, patriotically, and under conditions comparable to that of men, should have received pay privileges for that service. The knowledge of these heart-breaking cases, the bitterness which some of these loyal, patriotic women felt, was one of the prime factors in my plan for a Women's Army Auxiliary Corps.

Last May I introduced my bill, H. R. 4906, calling for the establishment of a Women's Army Auxiliary Corps for service with the Army of the United States. It was referred to the Committee on Military Affairs of the House, and the Secretary of War was requested to make a report and submit his recommendations to the chairman of the committee.

In simple language, the bill provides for the voluntary enrollment of women of excellent character, in good physical health, between the ages of 21 and 45 years, and who are citizens of the United States, in the Women's Army Auxiliary Corps for service with the Army of the United States. The term of service is defined in the bill as being for 1 year, with the customary proviso that in time of war, or of national emergency the Secretary of War may, by order, extend the term of service to include the period of the war or national emergency, plus not to exceed 6 months.

The measure provides for a Director of the Corps, who shall receive a salary of $3,000 a year, together with other allowances in lieu of quarters, rations, and so forth, where such is not supplied. This is comparable to the pay of a major in our Army.

The Corps will be a uniformed organization and the Secretary of War is authorized to furnish such uniforms, insignia, and so forth, under the regulations now being used for our Army.

Medical and dental services, hospitalization, and burial allowances in case of death are provided.

In the event of injury in the line of duty, or of illness, members of the Corps would be entitled to the same benefits prescribed by law for civilian employees of the United States Government, such jurisdiction to rest in the United States Employees' Compensation Commission.

Members of the corps are not subject to court martial, but shall be subject to disciplinary regulations which the Secretary of War may prescribe. The officers of the General Staff feel that discipline can be maintained under such regulations, with the worst punishment being a bad conduct discharge, a discharge without honor.

At the present time the Interceptor Command of the United States Army is using about 6,000 women in the information or filter centers of that service. These women are volunteers, giving their services patriotically and un-selfishly. It is pointed out, however, that it is vital to efficiency and to safety that the Army have military control over such employees. To illustrate the point, at the present time if Mrs. Smith, who is a plotter in one of the stations, found that she could not be on duty tomorrow afternoon because of some family duty requiring her presence at home, she could call the station and say that she could not be there, and the Army authorities could do nothing about it. In the case of the Women's Army Auxiliary Corps its members would be on duty, under the discipline and control of the Army authorities just as a soldier would be at any time, day or night. The War Department feels that the aircraft-warning service is much too important to leave to voluntary service without strict military control. If women are to be used on a military basis, you have got to have military control. The information and filter centers are highly organized installations, and a large part of the work done there can be done better, according to experts, by women than by men. It is a service in which speed is the prime essential—where a matter of a few seconds may mean the difference between life and death. In Great Britain it has been demonstrated time and again that women are faster, more alert, in this work than is the case with their brothers. Thus it is extremely essential that irregular attendance and excessive turn-over in personnel be eliminated in time of war in order to have a perfectly functioning, smooth organization under strict military control.

In addition to the needs of the Aircraft Warning Service, the members of the Women's Army Auxiliary Corps could be assigned as clerks, machine operators, telephone, telegraph, teletype, and switchboard operators, pharmacists, dieticians, hostesses, librarians, theater employees, welfare workers, post exchange employees, cooks, stewardesses, laundry workers, and messengers, or in any capacity which is noncombatant.

In talking with a high-ranking officer of our Army the other day about this bill, he pointed out to me that the one task his enlisted men disliked most was that of telephone operator. It is definitely a women's work and men admittedly do not make good operators as a rule. In many camps, located far from urban districts, it is almost impossible to use women for the work because of the lack of transportation facilities to bring them to their work and return them at the close of the day. Under the set-up proposed, the Women's Army Auxiliary Corps would take over the task and the members of the corps would live in quarters assigned to them on the post, under strict military control.

I wish with all my heart I could read to you many of the letters I have received. They are so sincere, so patriotic, so eager. One of them is typical, and I will read a part of it here:

"MY DEAR MRS. ROGERS: I have read and watched with a great deal of interest the comments and discussions concerning your bill for a Women's Army Auxiliary Corps, in fact I wrote to the War Department offering my services. I suppose the men think all we want is to get into a uniform. Perhaps they don't know that we realize the seriousness of the situation. They don't need to worry. I have a son, 16 years old in December, and all he talks of is getting in the Navy. I have a nephew on the Burma Road. I have two very dear cousins—handsome boys, over 6 feet tall—also two other people I love very much, who are in the Army in Florida. So I guess we women realize the situation and only want to help, and we can if we are allowed. During the World War, I took a man's place as a telegraph operator. After the depression I took up telephone operating, which I am now doing. I feel equal to instructing in either type of work. I hate this war and if we women can release men to fight why should we be held back? I wish you success. This is a poor effort to express what I feel, but I am sure there are plenty more who feel the same way."

If we are to have total war—and that is what we are experiencing at the present time—there is a very definite place for women in it. Modern war recognizes no limitations of battlefields, no gender of its participants. To win a total war every resource, every service must be utilized.

DOCUMENT 13

Richard R. Jefferson, "Negro Employment in St. Louis War Production." Opportunity 22, no. 3 (July–September 1944)

In July 1942, the Curtiss-Wright Company and the U.S. Cartridge Company announced that they would accept Negro applicants for training for skilled and semiskilled operators. By August the Curtiss-Wright Company had approximately 500 Negro workers in a segregated building on a variety of skilled jobs including welders, riveters, assemblers and inspectors.

Simultaneously, the U.S. Cartridge Company provided a segregated plant identical with other production units and employed a complete force of Negro production workers. . . .

At peak production the company employed a total of 4,500 Negroes, many of whom held jobs as machine operators, millwrights, inspectors, and adjusters.

If this form of segregation in industry can be looked upon with favor, it might be said that these firms made a reasonable effort to use the available Negro labor supply. However, other large industries attempted to restrict the number of Negroes to the population ratio of one to ten. Further, they made little or no effort to upgrade Negroes according to seniority or skills. This flat refusal to comply with the spirit and letter of the Executive Order has precipitated a very unsatisfactory situation and has caused numerous strikes and work stoppages among dissatisfied Negro workers. The prejudices of white workers in the area is usually blamed for the failure to upgrade Negroes. In at least 100 important war production plants no Negro workers have been employed.

The employment of Negro women in St. Louis industries presents a more discouraging picture as might be expected. Stronger resistance to their use except as maids and cleaners, or in segregated workshops, has been encountered in almost every instance. With the exception of the Curtiss-Wright Company which employs about 200 women as riveters, assemblers, and inspectors, and the U. S. Cartridge Company which used almost 1,000 women as operators and inspectors, few plants in the area have attempted to use them. The lack of separate toilet facilities and the prejudices of white women workers are the main barriers to the wider use of Negro women, according to officials of many of 200 plants that refuse to employ them.

Perhaps the one bright spot in this picture is the development in the garment industry, although the policy of segregation has been followed even in this field despite our efforts to eliminate it. Since 1930 the Urban League of St. Louis has worked to secure employment opportunities for Negro women in some of the numerous textile plants. In the Spring of 1941 the Acme Manufacturing Company opened an all-Negro plant employing 28 operators, a packer and a foreman. . . .

Until March, 1943, no other manufacturer would consider the employment of Negro women. With depleted labor reserves and mounting war orders, several plants were forced to look elsewhere for workers and the Portnoy Garment Company was one of the first to consider the use of Negroes. While not willing to integrate Negroes in the plant, the Portnoy Company agreed to open an all-Negro plant if a suitable building could be obtained and qualified workers were available. Because of the exclusion of Negroes from the trade, there were few if any experienced operators except those employed by the Acme Co. However, the St. Louis and East St. Louis N.Y.A. projects had given training to approximately 300 girls and a few had been trained at the Washington Technical School. From these groups, it was possible to recruit a sufficient number of operators to open the new plant on May 10, 1943. By the end of the year 60 women were employed and by May 1, 1944 the factory had 90 workers and was planning an expansion to accommodate an additional 40 operators. . . .

Negro workers in the St. Louis area have not accepted the discrimination against them without protest. Through mass meetings and petitions they have expressed their disapproval of the situation even after they secured employment. No less than a half dozen all-Negro strikes have occurred in protest against discriminatory hiring or working policies. In June, 1943, Negroes employed in the segregated plant of the U. S. Cartridge Company struck because the company would not upgrade qualified Negroes to jobs as foremen. The company finally agreed to comply with their demands. A few weeks later the workers in the segregated Curtiss-Wright staged a sit-down strike protesting the lack of adequate cooling equipment. In August, 1943, 600 Negro workers in the General Steel Castings plant in Madison, Illinois, struck because of a number of grievances including differentials in pay rates and discrimination against Negro women workers. After several weeks of negotiations in which the Urban League took an active part, 61 of the 62 grievance cases were satisfactorily adjusted.

In November, 1943 and March, 1944, 380 Negro employees of the Monsanto Chemical Company staged a series of work stoppages, one of which lasted 10 days. Long-standing grievances against both the company and the union were responsible for the difficulties, but the refusal to upgrade Negro workers was the major complaint. The League was instrumental in placing their grievances before company and union officials and an acceptable settlement was finally negotiated. Minor incidents involving the introduction and integration of Negro workers in the industries in this area have been too frequent to enumerate, and they have served to further confuse a very tense and unsettled war production center. . . .

Source: Rosalyn Baxandall, Linda Gordon, and Susan Reverby, *America's Working Women* (New York: Random House, 1976), 285–87.

DOCUMENT 14

"Women Workers in Ten War Production Areas and Their Postwar Employment Plans." Bulletin No. 209, Women's Bureau, 1946.

That very large numbers of wartime women workers intend to work after the war is evidenced by their statements to interviewers. On the average, about 75 percent of the wartime-employed women in the 10 areas expected to be part of the postwar labor force. . . .

These prospective postwar women workers did not, for the most part, contemplate out-migration from their areas of wartime employment. Over 90 percent of them, in most areas, looked forward to continued employment after the

Source: Rosalyn Baxandall, Linda Gordon and Susan Reverby, *America's Working Women* (New York: Random House, 1976), 310–312.

war in the same areas where they had worked during the war period. . . .

In each area, the number of wartime-employed women who intended to work in the same area after the war greatly exceeded the number of women employed in the area in 1940. . . .

The highest percentage of prospective post-war workers in most areas came from the group of women who had been employed before Pearl Harbor, rather than from those who had been in school or engaged in their own housework at that time. On the average over four-fifths of the women who had been employed both before Pearl Harbor and in the war period intended to keep on working after the war. Among the war-employed women who had not been in the labor force the week before Pearl Harbor, over three-fourths of the former students expected to continue working, while over half of those formerly engaged in their own housework had such plans. . . .

Very large proportions of the in-migrant women workers planned to continue work in the areas where they had been employed during the war. . . .

The nature of post-war employment problems is influenced not only by the number of wartime workers who expect to remain in the labor force but also by their expressed desires for work in particular industries and occupations. Post-war job openings as cafeteria bus girls, for example, are not apt to prove attractive to women who are seeking work as screw-machine operators.

The bulk of the prospective post-war workers interviewed in this survey, or 86 percent, wanted their post-war jobs in the same industrial group as their wartime employment, and about the same proportion wanted to remain in the same occupational group. Post-war shifts to other industries were contemplated on a somewhat larger scale, however, among the wartime employees in restaurants, cafeterias, and similar establishments, as well as in the personal service industries in certain areas. In the Dayton area, for example, among the war-employed women who expected to remain in the labor force, fully 36 percent of those in eating and drinking places and 30 percent of those in personal service industries said they wanted jobs in other industries after the war. . . .

In the Mobile area almost a third of the women employed in the war period were Negro. In four other areas between 10 and 19 percent, inclusive, were non-white (including some oriental in San Francisco). In the remaining five areas less than 10 percent of the war-employed women were Negro or of other non-white races.

In each of the nine areas where there were enough non-white employed women in the war period to make comparison valid, a much higher proportion of the Negro women planned to continue work than of the white women. In six areas 94 percent or more of the Negro or other non-white women who were employed in the war period planned to continue after the war. . . .

Responsibility for the support of themselves or themselves and others was the outstanding reason given by war-employed women for planning to continue work after the war. As already pointed out, about three-fourths of the wartime-employed women in the 10 areas (excluding household employees) planned to keep on working after the war. Fully 84 percent of them had no other alternative, as this was the proportion among them who based their decision on their need to support themselves and often, other persons as well. Eight percent offered special reasons for continuing at work, such as buying a home or sending children to school; and only 8 percent reported they would remain in the labor force because they liked working, or liked having their own money. . . .

That the need to work is just as pressing among some married women as among some single women was highlighted by the replies from the war-employed women on the number of wage earners in the family group. Out of every 100 married women who were living in family groups of two or more persons, 11 said they were the only wage earner supporting the family group. This was almost identical to the proportion of sole supporting wage earners among single women living with their families. The state of marriage, therefore, does not, in itself, always mean there is a male provider for the family. . . .

Chapter 6

The Resurgence of Feminism

Several components of earlier feminist thought, particularly the demand for equality before the law and equal opportunity in education and the professions, became prominent once again in the resurgence of organized feminism which took place during the 1960s. New issues as well became part of the feminist agenda. Feminists now insisted that in order to break down the barrier between the "public" and "private" spheres of activity, not only did women need to move into the public world, but men had to take more responsibility for the quality and conduct of domestic life. They also placed more emphasis on sexual freedom and expression than all but a handful of earlier feminists had done. In addition, increasing numbers of black and other minority women recorded and analyzed their own experiences and showed how feminism had to take account of race and class, as well as gender oppression.

Jo Freeman has distinguished two "branches" of the women's movement of the 1960s, the "older branch" and the "younger branch." (Freeman, 1975, 44–70) As Freeman is quick to note, these groups were not mutually exclusive, and did not think of themselves as "older" and "younger." But the terms are useful, pointing to the fact that contemporary feminism is made up both of the traditional emphasis on equality before the law and of more radical calls for new life styles and sexual mores, and that it attracted not only young women who came of age during and after the late 1960s but many women of earlier generations as well.

The older branch was initially made up largely of women active in government, business, or the professions, who began to press for greater equality of opportunity for women. Spurred by Eleanor Roosevelt and Esther Peterson (Assistant Secretary of Labor), President John Kennedy appointed a Commission on the Status of Women in 1961 to study and report on the legal impediments to women's advancement and to recommend changes. Both Peterson, who as newly-appointed head of the Women's Bureau supported protective labor legislation, and Kennedy, who was indebted to labor unions for his election, hoped that constructive recommendations for women's advancement might lay to rest the irksome issue of the Equal Rights Amendment. The Commission's *Report*, issued in 1963, rejected the ERA, but it did document and denounce widespread discrimination against women in marriage law, credit and housing regulations, and educational practices. Since many of these matters were under the jurisdiction of state legislatures, after 1963 state commissions on the status of women were established to propose changes in state laws necessary to insure equality. Some of the members of the state commissions, however, wanted to move faster than did the federal bureaucracy. At the Third National Conference of Commissions on the Status of Women, a group of delegates proposed a resolution urging the Equal Employment Opportunity Commission (EEOC) to enforce the prohibition on sex discrimination contained in Title VII of the Civil Rights Act of 1964 as vigorously as it did the prohibition on race discrimination. The chairperson, not wishing to embarrass the EEOC, ruled on technical grounds that the resolution was out of order. That evening, a group of disgruntled delegates met in a hotel room to form the National Organization for Women (NOW).

The concerns of NOW, and more generally of the "older branch" of contemporary feminism are reflected in the 1967 NOW Bill of Rights. [See Document 15] NOW members no longer saw the Equal Rights Amendment as a threat to women's well-being, and endorsed it. The next five titles all had to do with educational and employment opportunities, and with several proposals dealing with maternity and child-care benefits for working mothers. The seventh dealt with the rights of women in poverty to financial support and personal dignity, and the final one demanded the repeal of laws prohibiting abortion. Comparing the NOW Bill of Rights to the Declaration of Sentiments of Seneca Falls and the 1936 Women's Charter shows how central to American feminism has been the demand for legal equality. At Seneca Falls attention centered on suffrage and on married women's disabilities; NOW's endorsement of an ERA (this was five years before Congress passed the Amendment and sent it to the states for ratification) indicated that the vote alone had not been able to insure equitable treatment for women. If this was the greatest continuity, the most striking new demand was for the legalization of abortion (which would be realized in the 1973 Supreme Court decision *Roe* v. *Wade*). The nineteenth century feminists had advocated women's control over reproduction, but through what they called "voluntary motherhood," a woman's right to limit sexual intercourse to times when she desired conception. Members of the women's movement differed deeply over the morality and advisability of abortion, but most agreed that for government to prohibit or attach criminal sanctions to abortion was an illegitimate intrusion on women's privacy.

Using legal reform to achieve sex equality characterized the older branch of the new feminism, while activities such as consciousness-raising sessions, protest demonstrations, and "for women only" social and cultural events were typical of the younger branch. The younger branch grew out of the civil rights, student and anti-war movements of the 1960s. The resurgence of feminism was particularly indebted to the civil rights movement both for the attention it focused on equality under the law, and for the political experience women gained in the movement. At the same time, however, young women engaged in each of these movements experienced discrimination akin to that which abolitionist women had felt. Engaged in voter registration drives in the South, or helping to organize Students for a Democratic Society (SDS), or working at draft resistance counseling, women found that they were repeatedly relegated to clerical, rather than policy-making, tasks. They also complained that they were frequently identified by their sex function, even when engaged in political work. Two public instances of this tendancy were Stokely Carmichel's response to a question concerning women's position in the Student Non-Violent Coordinating Committee (SNCC) that "The position of women in SNCC is prone," and a slogan used by the New England Draft Resistance, "Girls say 'yes' to guys who say 'no'." Partly in protest against this trivialization of their political concerns many young women began to form women's caucuses within existing organizations, and then to identify women's liberation itself as a goal and a political movement.

"Women's liberation" implied somewhat different goals than "women's rights." The latter required legal changes. "Liberation" suggested changes in areas outside the law: personal self-confidence and self-reliance, greater sexual freedom, the end of the sex-role based division of labor. One of the tools developed to foster women's liberation was consciousness-raising (C.R.) groups, where a small number of women would meet to share their experiences with a view of seeing how their own behavior or societal expectations kept them from doing what they wanted or might be able to accomplish. One great asset of consciousness-raising was that it uncovered many areas where women saw that they had very similar experiences, and it helped them to see that problems which they had regarded as idiosyncratic and due to their personal failure were common to many women. These discoveries gave rise to the popular phrase, "the personal is the political." One popular essay, Pat Mainardi's "The Politics of Housework," published in Robin Morgan's *Sisterhood Is Powerful*, pointed out that the trivialization of women's work and women's concerns was in itself a powerful tool of their subordination.

The new women's movement also built up networks of female support and friendship, which sometimes served to encourage women to try new jobs, political activities, and personal relationships. The C.R. groups were decentralized and autonomous, often formed spontaneously within a network of friends or in a workplace, school or neighborhood. Despite the wide disparity of aims and interests, however, the groups did instill a sense of community and of female solidarity. This aspect of feminism found early expression in the "Redstockings' Manifesto," issued by the Redstockings collective in Boston. [See Document 16]

The 1970s saw a number of notable successes for feminists, followed by an intense, virulent, and politically sophisticated backlash. In 1971 the Supreme Court struck new ground in sex discrimination litigation when it decided in *Reed* v. *Reed* that "administrative convenience" was not sufficient justification for a statutory preference for men rather than women as administrators of estates. This ruling opened the way for a series of important decisions which developed the Equal Protection Clause of the Fourteenth Amendment as a tool for obtaining equal statutory treatment for women and men. (In one of these cases, *Frontiero* v. *Richardson*, four justices wanted to go so far as to declare sex a "suspect classification" like race, alienage and national origin, although a majority declined to do so.) In 1972 Congress submitted the Equal Rights Amendment to the states for ratification. In 1973 the Supreme Court handed down the highly controversial decision permitting abortions, *Roe* v. *Wade*. At the same time feminists began to institutionalize their gains and their concerns. The Feminist Press was founded to publish new and out-of-print works by women; *MS.* magazine began publication in 1972; the scholarly journals *Feminist Studies* and *Signs* appeared in 1972 and 1975. Organizations like NOW, the National Black Feminist Organization, and the National Women's Political Caucus increased their memberships. Over five hundred campuses inaugurated Women's Studies programs and some twenty research centers concerning women and gender existed by the mid-1970s; by 1982 there were some 30,000 women's studies courses offered at American colleges and universities.

All this activity stimulated a backlash from those who felt that feminism threatened traditional sex roles, family stability, and certain Judeo-Christian moral principles. The politically most powerful opposition to feminists came from New Right organizations like the Moral Majority. Labelling themselves part of a "pro-family" movement, such groups attempted to keep sex-education out of the public schools (claiming it would result in female sexual promiscuity), block ratification of the Equal Rights Amendment (claiming it would drive married women from their homes and into the paid labor force), and introduce both statutes and Constitutional amendments which would prohibit or severely restrict access to abortions. The anti-feminism implicit in much of the New Right's program has been analyzed in such essays as Zillah Eisenstein, "Antifeminism in the Politics and Election of 1980," and Rosalind Petchesky, "Antiabortion, Antifeminism and the Rise of the New Right," both in *Feminist Studies* Vol. 7, (Summer 1981).

The nomination of Geraldine Ferraro as the Vice-Presidential candidate of the Democratic Party in 1984 testified to the changes in American politics produced in part by the contemporary feminist movement. Women were perceived as a politicized constituency whose interests could only be ignored with peril. While the appearance of a woman on the Democratic national ticket was of great symbolic importance, it by no means signaled the resolution of feminist political struggles. For example, feminists continued to stress the need for equal employment opportunity and equal compensation for working women. "Comparable worth," that is, paying men and women equally for comparable but not identical jobs, became a goal of the continuing struggle for pay equity and a means for overcoming the devaluation of women's jobs. Feminist discussions of public policy in the 1980s also grappled with the dual roles of family member and worker, of private and public person, which men and women assumed in increasing numbers as more and more women entered the labor force. Thus questions of how the hours of work might be better structured to allow women and men alike to meet their family obligations, how to provide quality child-care, and how to provide parental leaves became as prevalent and pressing as those concerning how to insure strict legal equality between men and women in the public sphere.

The need for serious thinking about the needs of families and children was particularly acute because of the "feminization" of poverty. In 1981 two-thirds of the long-term poor were women, and the National Advisory Council on Economic Opportunity predicted that if present trends continued, by the year 2000 *all* of the poor in the United States would be women and children in female-headed households. Clearly, family life could not be regarded as exclusively a "private" matter without disastrous consequences, particularly for children.

The struggle for women's equality in the United States repeatedly pitted the image of woman as mother and homemaker against that of woman as worker and active citizen. Feminist activists of both sexes rejected that dichotomy in the 1980s, and undertook the restructuring of public and private life to accomodate easier movement back and forth between these complementary spheres of human activity. Whether and how their efforts will bear fruit in public policy and daily life will affect the quality of both political and family life in the United States.

The relationship of black women to feminism throughout the course of the contemporary movement has been complex. Black women were active in the movements from which the new feminists arose, particularly civil rights organizations. Black women produced some powerful early works of feminist analysis, among them Pauli Murray's "The Liberation of Black Women" in Mary Lou Thompson, ed., *Voices of the New Feminism* (1970), Toni Cade, ed., *The Black Woman: An Anthology* (1970) and essays collected in Gerda Lerner, ed., *Black Women in White America: A Documentary History* (1972). These works were particularly important because they stressed the double oppression of race and of sex. Many black women suffered from segregation, poverty, inadequate public services, and social hostility on account of race. Additionally, they suffered from sexual stereotypes and were dismissed as less "serious" and "important" members of the community by some whites and blacks alike due to their sex. Some blacks particularly felt the irony of having to rely on the black woman for much of the family income because of high rates of black male unemployment, only to find themselves criticized for not conforming to the "normal" family pattern of male breadwinner and stay-at-home wife.

Despite the common ground which black and white women shared with regard to sex role stereotyping and sexual exploitation, in the mid-1970s some black feminists became increasingly impatient with and alienated from the major organizations of the feminist movement. One frequently-heard explanation for this was that feminists did not pay attention to poor women; that they were middle-class, college-educated, aspiring professionals who wanted their piece of the pie of privilege and affluence. But many black feminists were themselves middle-class. The source of alienation was deeper, and included resentment of white feminists' appropriation of the rhetoric of racial discrimination. There were of course some analogies between race and sex discrimination: both attached to involuntary and immutable characteristics; both historically closed the doors to schools and profes-

sions; and both could be psychologically as well as materially damaging. On the other hand, middle-class white women were not ghettoized as were blacks, but lived in close intimacy with men, and shared indirectly in the social status and wealth of their men. As many black women pointed out, equating discrimination against women with discrimination against blacks made the difficulties of middle-class white women aspiring to a profession the prototype of "victimization." And in comparing the situations of "blacks" on the one hand and "women" on the other, it suggested that these were two distinct groups, ignoring the dual identity of black women. The late 1970s saw the publication of a number of works by black feminists such as Bell Hooks, *Ain't I a Woman* and Angela Davis, *Women, Race and Class* which insisted upon a more careful analysis of different mechanisms of discrimination and different kinds of oppression facing black and white women in the United States. Women of other racial minorities, like Native Americans, also gave voice to their experiences as women living in a culture which they perceived as alien both because it was male-dominated and because it was predominantly white. [Document 17]

Another aspect of women's liberation which drew some women of all races into political activity was the struggle for gay or lesbian rights. [See Document 18] Lesbianism was, of course, not a new phenomenon, but lesbians had not previously insisted upon the *public* recognition of their right to love whomever they chose, and protections against discrimination due to sexual preference. The lesbian rights movement had ties to both the movement for personal and sexual liberation of the 1960s, and the various movements for civil rights for minorities and oppressed groups. Some lesbians asserted that by continuing to live with men and sharing in the economic and social privileges which men gave them, "straight" women fell short in their commitment to other women. Some straight women, for their part, tried to downplay the links between lesbian rights and other women's issues because they thought lesbianism would undercut support for other women's causes. By the 1980s, however, many of the splits between lesbian and straight women had diminished. Feminists, regardless of sexual orientation, generally tended to support lesbian rights not only out of a commitment to the liberal principle of toleration, but because they recognized all too well that attacks on lesbians divided and demeaned all women.

Some men as well as women joined the feminist movement. Some did so out of a commitment to social and particularly legal equality. Other men became feminists not simply in support of *women's* rights, but because of their own experience of the oppressive nature of men's traditional roles in American society. They pointed out how burdensome it could be to be solely responsible for the family income and most of its social status, to be deprived of any meaningful involvement in child-rearing, and to be socially ridiculed for displays of deep feeling perfectly acceptable in women. Many people began to talk of the "women's liberation movement" as a movement for "human liberation," which would redefine not only appropriate sex roles but the modes in which people would deal with one another, replacing hierarchy and subordination with greater equality and reciprocity.

Beginning in the latter part of the 1970s, however, the international feminist movement called into question the scope and breadth of American feminism's commitment to universal "human" liberation. At the 1975 International Women's Year Conference in Mexico City, the 1980 Mid-

Decade Women's Conference in Copenhagen, and the Nairobi Conference of 1985, "Third World" women challenged what they perceived as North American women's narrow-minded concentration on equal political, legal and economic rights, particularly on professional employment opportunities. Women from Asia, Africa and Latin America had instead concerned themselves with development, hunger, education, and health care for both men and women in their countries. The anthology *Sisterhood Is Global*, edited by Robin Morgan, captured the range of feminist concerns and perspectives found worldwide.

Conclusion

Women's relationship to political life in the United States has a complex and multifaceted history. One aspect of that history has been women's persistent effort to expand their participation in politics. The suffrage movement was perhaps the most prominent part of this movement, but it was only one of a multitude of ways in which women entered public life. Women participated in the abolitionist, temperance, and antilynching campaigns of the nineteenth century. They undertook a multitude of activities as "social feminists" during the Progressive Era. Women were increasingly appointed to a wide variety of public offices, and they moved up in the ranks of the political parties in the 1920s and '30s. Many entered the military services during World War II. Women participated in the civil rights, anti-war, environmental, pro-choice, anti-abortion, and other political movements of the 1960s, '70s and '80s. They campaigned for elective office at the local, state and national level. These endeavors reflect the wide variety of ways in which women have sought to influence the conduct of public life and to expand their roles as citizens.

A second feature of women's political history in the United States has been the continuous struggle to guarantee women and men equal rights under the law. That goal, of course, involved gaining the suffrage, but it encompassed many other efforts as well. In nearly all the states feminists have worked to amend state laws concerning divorce, access to higher education, married women's property, child custody, equal pay, equal employment opportunity, and a plethora of other measures. In the 1970s, lawyers increasingly used the Fourteenth and Fifteenth Amendments to the U.S. Constitution to give women the "equal protection" of the law. The effort to add an Equal Rights Amendment to the Constitution began in 1923 and has continued to the present day.

Throughout all these efforts to expand their participation in public life and secure their legal rights, feminists have analyzed the nature of politics, and of men's and women's roles in a democratic society. One of the purposes of this book has been to show how substantial, long-lived, and vital the feminist tradition of political thought in the United States has been. Feminist writings include the "Declaration" and "Resolutions" adopted at Seneca Falls; the works of Elizabeth Cady Stanton, Ida B. Wells, Charlotte Perkins Gilman, Jane Addams, Emma Goldman, Mary Inman, Margaret Sanger, Mary Beard and many others; newspapers like *Revolution*, *Woman's Journal*, *Suffragist*, and *Equal Rights*; magazines and journals in our own day like *Off Our Backs*, *Ms.*, *Signs*, and *Feminist Studies*.

The effort to analyze and assess women's relationship to political life will undoubtedly continue as men and women alike seek to understand the meaning and implications of sexual equality for life in a democratic polity. Such equality would transform aspects not only of public life, but of personal life as well. The feminist tradition in the United States is a source of inspiration and strength for present-day activists working to further the centuries-old goals of human dignity, liberty, and equality for women.

DOCUMENT 15

NOW (National Organization for Women) Bill of Rights

Adopted at NOW's first national conference, Washington, D.C., 1967.

I. Equal Rights Constitutional Amendment.

II. Enforce Law Banning Sex Discrimination in Employment.

III. Maternity Leave Rights in Employment and in Social Security Benefits.

IV. Tax Deduction for Home and Child Care Expenses for Working Parents.

V. Child Day Care Centers.

VI. Equal and Unsegregated Education.

VII. Equal Job Training Opportunities and Allowances for Women in Poverty.

VIII. The Right of Women to Control Their Reproductive Lives.

WE DEMAND:

I. That the U.S. Congress immediately pass the Equal Rights Amendment to the Constitution to provide that "Equality of rights under the law shall not be denied or abridged by the United States or by any State on account of sex," and that such then be immediately ratified by the several States.

II. That equal employment opportunity be guaranteed to all women, as well as men, by insisting that the Equal Employment Opportunity Commission enforces the prohibitions against sex discrimination in employment under Title VII of the Civil Rights Act of 1964 with the same vigor as it enforces the prohibitions against racial discrimination.

III. That women be protected by law to ensure their rights to return to their jobs within a reasonable time after childbirth without loss of seniority or other accrued benefits, and be paid maternity leave as a form of social security and/or employee benefit.

IV. Immediate revision of tax laws to permit the deduction of home and child-care expenses for working parents.

V. That child-care facilities be established by law on the same basis as parks, libraries, and public schools, adequate to the needs of children from the pre-school years through adolescence, as a community resource to be used by all citizens from all income levels.

VI. That the right of women to be educated to their full potential equally with men be secured by Federal and State legislation, eliminating all discrimination and segregation by sex, written and unwritten, at all levels of education, including colleges, graduate and professional schools, loans and fellowships, and Federal and State training programs such as the Job Corps.

VII. The right of women in poverty to secure job training, housing, and family allowances on equal terms with men, but without prejudice to a parent's right to

Source: Robin Morgan, ed., Sisterhood is Powerful, New York: Random House, 1970.

remain at home to care for his or her children; revision of welfare legislation and poverty programs which deny women dignity, privacy, and self-respect.

VIII. The right of women to control their own reproductive lives by removing from the penal code laws limiting access to contraceptive information and devices, and by repealing penal laws governing abortion.

DOCUMENT 16

Redstockings Manifesto

I. After centuries of individual and preliminary political struggle, women are uniting to achieve their final liberation from male supremacy. Redstockings is dedicated to building this unity and winning our freedom.

II. Women are an oppressed class. Our oppression is total, affecting every facet of our lives. We are exploited as sex objects, breeders, domestic servants, and cheap labor. We are considered inferior beings, whose only purpose is to enhance men's lives. Our humanity is denied. Our prescribed behavior is enforced by the threat of physical violence.

Because we have lived so intimately with our oppressors, in isolation from each other, we have been kept from seeing our personal suffering as a political condition. This creates the illusion that a woman's relationship with her man is a matter of interplay between two unique personalities, and can be worked out individually. In reality, every such relationship is a *class* relationship, and the conflicts between individual men and women are *political* conflicts that can only be solved collectively.

III. We identify the agents of our oppression as men. Male supremacy is the oldest, most basic form of domination. All other forms of exploitation and oppression (racism, capitalism, imperialism, etc.) are extensions of male supremacy: men dominate women, a few men dominate the rest. All power structures throughout history have been male-dominated and male-oriented. Men have controlled all political, economic and cultural institutions and backed up this control with physical force. They have used their power to keep women in an inferior position. *All men* receive economic, sexual and psychological benefits from male supremacy. *All men* have oppressed women.

IV. Attempts have been made to shift the burden of responsibility from men to institutions or to women themselves. We condemn these arguments as evasions. Institutions alone do not oppress; they are merely tools of the oppressor. To blame institutions implies that men and women are equally victimized, obscures the fact that men benefit from the subordination of women, and gives men the excuse that they are forced to be oppressors. On the contrary, any man is free to renounce his superior position provided that he is willing to be treated like a woman by other men.

We also reject the idea that women consent to or are to blame for their own oppression. Women's submission is not the result of brainwashing, stupidity, or mental illness but of continual, daily pressure from men. We do not need to change ourselves, but to change men.

The most slanderous evasion of all is that women can oppress men. The basis for this illusion is the isolation of individual relationships from their political context and the tendency of men to see any legitimate challenge to their privileges as persecution.

V. We regard our personal experience, and our feelings about that experience, as the basis for an analysis of our common situation. We cannot rely on existing ideologies as they are all products of male supremacist culture. We question every generalization and accept none that are not confirmed by our experience.

Our chief task at present is to develop female class consciousness through sharing experience and publicly exposing the sexist foundation of all our institutions. Consciousness-raising is not "therapy," which implies the existence of individual solutions and falsely assumes that the male-female relationship is purely personal, but the only method by which we can ensure that our program for liberation is based on the concrete realities of our lives.

The first requirement for raising class consciousness is honesty, in private and in public, with ourselves and other women.

VI. We identify with all women. We define our best interest as that of the poorest, most brutally exploited woman.

We repudiate all economic, racial, educational or status privileges that divide us from other women. We are determined to recognize and eliminate any prejudices we may hold against other women.

We are committed to achieving internal democracy. We will do whatever is necessary to ensure that every woman in our movement has an equal chance to participate, assume responsibility, and develop her political potential.

VII. We call on all our sisters to unite with us in struggle.

We call on all men to give up their male privileges and support women's liberation in the interest of our humanity and their own.

In fighting for our liberation we will always take the side of women against their oppressors. We will not ask what is "revolutionary" or "reformist," only what is good for women.

The time for individual skirmishes has passed. This time we are going all the way.

July 7, 1969

REDSTOCKINGS
P.O. Box 748
Stuyvesant Station
New York, N.Y. 10009

DOCUMENT 17

"Taking Stock of Where We've Been . . . And Where We're At: Past Positives/Present Problems"

Shirley Hill Witt (Akwesasne Mohawk), Director, Rocky Mountain Regional Office, U.S. Commission on Civil Rights

Living in Two Worlds

There is no Native person in North America who is untouched by the Anglo world, the White man's world, the American way. Nor are any of us immune to its infectiousness. Yet few self-identifying American Indians

Source: Leslie B. Tanner, *Voices from Women's Liberation*, (New York: New American Library, 1970).

Source: *Words of Today's Indian Women: Ohoyo Makachi* (Wichita Falls, Texas: Ohoyo Resource Center, 1982), 11–14.

live exclusively in the non-Indian world. To be "Indian" carries for many a sense of homeland (reservation, tribe, community) and duty to one's people, no matter where one currently resides . . . or whether one ever returns . . . or whether those duties are ever discharged. Thus Native peoples are aware of and practice to varying degrees two, often widely contrasting, life-styles. To move between these two worlds can be a feast of appreciation for human ingenuity, or it can be the bitterest trap.

Whether they live in an apartment in Minneapolis or attend the Bureau of Indian Affairs School on the San Juan Pueblo in New Mexico, Indian children typically learn two sets of ways—neither of them perfectly. *No* human knows his or her own culture perfectly, but what one culture has created is certainly learnable by members of another and is limited only by our intelligence and our opportunity to learn. And so, most Native people nowadays grow up with a two-track cultural background and find themselves participating to greater or lesser extent both in the Indian world as defined by their tribal affiliation, and in the White man's world. This term, "The White man's world," by the way, is not to be taken as a quaint archaic phrase: the world of the White *woman* is, for the most part, invisible to Indians. Even if it weren't invisible, it is irrelevent, since the White *man's* world is the one making an impact upon Indian life and Indian individuals. It is still the Great White Father (sic), who determines the quality of life for Native people as well as all other Americans, male and female.

From Strength Before Columbus

As many as 280 distinct aboriginal societies existed in North America prior to Columbus. *Not* surprisingly, some tribes practiced the oppression of women by men. But, in several, the roles of Native women stand in stark contrast to those of Europeans. These societies were matriarchal, matrilineal, and matrilocal—which is to say that women largely controlled family matters, inheritance passed through the female lines and upon marriage the bride usually brought her groom into her mother's household.

In a matrilocal household, all the women were blood relatives and all the males were outsiders. This sort of residence pattern was frequently seen among agricultural societies in which women bore the responsibility for farming while the men went off to do the hunting. It guaranteed a close-knit working force of women who had grown up with each other and with the land.

Although the lives of Native American women differed greatly from tribe to tribe, oftentimes their life-styles exhibited a great deal more independence and security than those of the European women who came to these shores. Indian women, in many cases, had individual freedom within tribal life that women in so-called "advanced" societies were not to experience for generations. Furthermore—and in contrast—Native women *increased* in value in the estimation of their society as they grew older. Their cumulative wisdom was considered one of society's most valuable resources.

New Native Women Speak: Past Positives/Present Problems

In recent years I have sought out successful Native women to find out how they have achieved their current levels of success in the Indian world, or the Anglo world, or both. I have asked them about how things were for women in their grandmother's lives and in their own. And, finally, I have asked them to tell me about themselves

today, about the problems and the victories they have experienced.

What I will be sharing with you for the remainder of my talk will be the words and thoughts of these women, as best as I could capture their ideas on paper.

Traditional vs. Modern Roles

What were the joys and the conflicts between traditional vs. modern roles? Options for women in the past have been limited for *all* cultures, given the reality of women's biology and the limited control women have had over determining pregnancy. Thelma Stiffarm (Gros Ventre/Cree) observed that, "In my mother's generation it was expected that the women would stay home and raise the children. My generation has conflict when remembering how nice it was growing up with my mother always there. I don't know if it was *Indian* culture or *White* culture, since *all* women stayed home then." Rain Parrish (Navajo) said, "Traditionally, every woman should have a child. Females were to give birth, to give life." But Bella McCabe, also a Navajo, feels that whereas not all sheep and goats are good mothers, not all *women* are made to be mothers. There are other important roles for them to play instead. The traditional roles of Native women often extended far beyond the hogan or tipi door. "In my tribe," says Stiffarm, "Indian women were always given the opportunity to do whatever they wanted and were always encouraged to do so. We've always had Indian tribal councilwomen. We had women warriors." McCabe reports that in Navajo life, "It's a woman's land and everything is centered around the woman. If anyone is oppressed, it's the Navajo men." . . . McCabe says, "Indian men recognize the necessity for some wives to work: it's no problem, and anyone who knows how to should handle the money. I do it all in my family. Most of the women in Navajo families handle the money. My grandmother always had her purse with the family money on a string under her skirt."

While the traditional cultures viewed women's roles as primarily being involved in family and household needs, many tribal groups expected women to play key roles in the political and religious areas of Native life. As Stiffarm indicated, some even had women warriors such as those known as the "brave-hearted women" among the Dakota, one reincarnate today being an organization called W.A.R.N. (Women of All Red Nations) to serve the needs of their people. Movement into the Anglo world of work and education is seen as necessary, or an opportunity. It is not *necessarily* seen as a major treat to traditional concepts of women's behavior.

DOCUMENT 18

Martha Shelly, "Notes of a Radical Lesbian"

Lesbianism is one road to freedom—freedom from oppression by men.

To see Lesbianism in this context—as a mode of living neither better nor worse than others, as one which offers its own opportunities—one must abandon the notion that deviance from the norm arises from personal illnesses.

Source: Robin Morgan, ed., *Sisterhood is Powerful* (New York: Vantage, 1970).

When members of the Women's Liberation Movement picketed the 1968 Miss America pageant, the most terrible epithet heaped on our straight sisters was "Lesbian." The sisters faced hostile audiences who called them "commies," and "tramps," but some of them broke into tears when they were called Lesbians. When a woman showed up at a feminist meeting and announced that she was a Lesbian, many women avoided her. Others told her to keep her mouth shut, for fear that she would endanger the cause. They felt that men could be persuaded to accept some measure of equality for women—as long as these women would parade their devotion to heterosexuality and motherhood.

Men fear Lesbians because they are less dependent, and because their hostility is less controlled.

Straight women fear Lesbians because of the Lesbian inside them, because we represent an alternative. They fear us for the same reason that uptight middle-class people fear hip people. They are angry at us because we have a way out that they are afraid to take.

And what happens to the Lesbian under all this pressure? Many of my sisters, confused by the barrage of anti-gay propaganda, have spent years begging to be allowed to live. They have come begging because they believed they were psychic cripples, and that other people were healthy and had the moral right to judge them. Many have lived in silence, burying themselves in their careers, like name-changing Jews or blacks who passed for white. Many have retreated into an apolitical domesticity, concerning themselves only with the attempt to maintain a love relationship in a society which attempts to destroy love and replace it with consumer goods, and which attempts to completely destroy any form of love outside the monogamous marriage.

Because Lesbian has become such a vile epithet, we have been afraid to fight openly. We can lose our jobs; we have fewer civil rights than any other minority group. Because we have few family ties and no children, for the most part, we have been active in many causes, but always in secret, because our name contaminates any cause that we work for.

To the radical Lesbian, I say that we can no longer afford to fight for everyone else's cause while ignoring our own. Ours is a life-style born out of a sick society; so is everyone else's. Our kind of love is as valid as anyone else's. The revolution must be fought for us, too, not only for blacks, Indians, welfare mothers, grape pickers, SDS people, Puerto Ricans, or mine workers. We must have a revolution for *human rights*. If we are in a bag, it's as good as anyone else's bag.

Epilogue

A Liberation Ideology:
The Intersection of Race, Sex, and Class
by Shelby Lewis

In an article entitled "Exit Visa from the World System: Dilemmas of Cultural and Economic Disengagement," Ali Mazrui provides an interesting analysis of alternative responses of Third World nations to global capitalist domination and exploitation. He examines strategies and consequences of obtaining visas for entering and participating in the global system and he examines strategies and consequences of obtaining visas for exiting the global capitalist system. (Mazrui, 1981)

Mazrui reaches four significant conclusions about the relationship between Third World nations and the global system which dominates and exploits them. One, he argues that unconditional entry into the global system amounts to complete surrender to west-hegemony; two, he maintains that total exit from the world system is impossible; three, he suggests that selective entry and participation in the system when combined with exits from selected areas of activity provides potential for some degree of disengagement; and four, he concludes that entry into the system simply to rearrange the furniture is problematic, at best. Entry must be gained with a view to renovating and reconstructing the system.

While Mazrui is vague about how a strategy of selective entry and exits is operationalized and his use of the visa as a symbol of disengagement is questionable, his analytical framework has some relevance for an analysis of the relationship between black American women and the larger American society. Clearly, black women would find it difficult to make a total break from American society at this point in time. But, it is equally clear that inclusion at any price is unacceptable. Therefore, a strategy of selective entry combined with selective exits with a view towards transformation of the system might be a workable alternative. But transformation in this context means fundamental change, not incrementalism. Transformation of the total society is revolution, not reform.

DuBois (1945), Cabral (1973), Davis (1982) and others suggest that individuals and groups with the least to lose from change and the most to gain by dismantling and reordering society are likely to generate and support revolutionary change. By any measure, it is obvious that black women have little to lose and much to gain by pursuing a revolutionary course toward liberation. But, are black women supportive of revolutionary transformation? Are black women generating revolutionary ideas,

organizations and liberating ideologies? What are the strategies for change utilized by black American women? What are the social, economic and political conditions and obstacles that black women face in a liberation struggle? This Epilogue attempts to address some of these questions.

Specifically I wish to examine the intersection of race, sex, and class in American society and analyze the conditions which are a consequence of this intersection. Since black women constitute the major group being victimized by this intersection, their material and social conditions will be examined with a view towards determining whether such conditions predispose them towards transformation and total liberation.

There is sufficient evidence to suggest that valid conclusions about change grow out of theory building and data analysis and that a comprehensive analysis of black American women must of necessity address the historical and contemporary linkages between them and African and Caribbean women. Black women in Atlanta, Kingston, Montreal, Addis Ababa and Nairobi are all victims of global racism, global sexism, and global capitalism. There are no national, regional, or continental boundaries to their oppression. Language, culture and national origin do not make a significant difference in their victimization. The oppressors may speak different tongues, but they speak an international language of oppression. (Lapchick and Urdang, 1982)

Certainly there are particularities of each group and of each struggle. And attempts to define and prescribe for another group's specific struggle should be discouraged. However, it should be understood that any approach to the question of liberation for related segments or groups bound together by history and a global system of oppression must reflect an awareness of the relationship and linkages between the whole and the parts. Thus, a provincial approach to the liberation of black American women is both unrealistic and irresponsible.

The oppression that women, workers/peasants, blacks, and other minorities face is a manifestation of global ethnocentricity, patriarchy and class bias; it is also a reflection of the many faces of imperialism. Black women, for example, are subjected to political, economic and cultural imperialism. As a powerless group they are dominated and ruled by others. Economically they are exploited and discriminated against by all other groups in American society. Culturally the values, codes and images of the dominant group(s) are imposed upon them and negative stereotyping results which further exacerbates their oppressive conditions. The combination of these factors leads to a permanent underclass status for black women in America, and liberation from these conditions becomes a matter of survival.

A logical first step in a liberation struggle of this nature would seem to be documentation and analysis of actual conditions facing black women. Once this is done, the development of a theory or framework for understanding, grounding, confronting, and changing those conditions is possible. This framework or theory should enable black women to formulate goals, objectives and strategies for changing their conditions. Implementation of the agreed on strategy growing out of the theory will not be easy, but life without freedom and justice is even more difficult to endure.

The Conditions of Black Women

Socio-economic, educational and psychological data on black women indicate their global permanent underclass status. Such data also illustrate that they are an integral part of and constitute large percentages of all oppressed groups, including poor people and peasants, women of all nations, Blacks—wherever they are found—and other minorities. They are often oppressed within these respective groupings. In a word, they are oppressed by other groups as well as by the major world oppressors—men and whites.

The conditions of black women are multi-dimensional, global, systemic, personal, and persistent. The many dimensions of their condition determine the nature of the struggle. Each dimension feeds on and exacerbates the other. The racism that confronts them is a major cause of poverty and poverty leads to further stratification and discrimination along class lines, and sexism leads to dependency and poverty especially for black women household heads. (Jones, 1982; Klein, 1980, Rodgers-Rose, 1980).

An examination of the economic plight of black American women reveals that they are constrained by a system of racist capitalist patriarchy. One indicator of the severity of the economic conditions of black women as a consequence of the intersection of race, sex and class is official government statistics on poverty in America. The following figures of the Department of Housing and Urban Development illustrate that black women who head households (over 55% of black females in central cities are household heads) are disproportionately poorer than other groups in the population.

Poverty Levels in American Households

Black Female-headed Households	51%
White Female-headed Households	27%
Black Male-headed Households	10.8%
White Male-headed Households	5.3%

The differences between poverty in white, male-headed households (5.3%) and black, female-headed households

Source: U.S. Department of Housing and Urban Development. *Female-Headed Households*. Government Printing Office, Washington, D.C., 1978.

(51%) is dramatic. The labor market is hierarchical, with men at the top and women at the bottom. The present status of women in the labor market and the current pattern of sex-segregated jobs is the result of a long process of interaction between patriarchy and capitalism. The relationship between poverty levels of blacks and whites, regardless of sex, is the result of a long process of interaction between racism and capitalism. The two separate relationships produce poverty and the most affected victim of a system where white racism and male chauvinism intersect is the black woman.

Both gender and race are important determinants of economic well being in America (Staples, 1973). Women and Blacks enter the labor market with distinct disadvantages. Their earning capabilities are handicapped by prejudice, institutional employment patterns, institutionalized racism and institutionalized chauvinism, and outright discrimination. They do not receive equal access or opportunities in the labor market, and they do not receive equal pay for equal work regardless of their educational training. (Suter and Miller, 1973).

It is important to point out that the underclass status of black women is an international phenomenon. The incidence of black female-headed households living in poverty is not limited to the central cities of North America. Both rural and urban black women in Africa and the Caribbean have higher incidences of gender isolation and poverty than other racial groups. For example, over 40% of the households in rural Botswana are headed by poor black women. The statistics are even higher for Lesotho and parts of Zimbabwe, Cape Verde, and South Africa, and in the Caribbean the problem is also acute. It is clear that this potent combination of sex, race and poverty is a global phenomenon. How black women respond to these conditions determines, in large part, their future and the future viability of racist capitalist patriarchy.

As a result of or in addition to being at the bottom of the economic ladder, black women have no political power in America. Currently only three black women serve on national legislative bodies and fewer than 1% of all state legislators are black women. (Prestage, 1980). They are too poor to buy power and too powerless to overcome poverty. Progress within the established system is unlikely given the rules and rulers. Revolution and transformation of the system appear to be the only avenues to liberation for black women.

Furthermore, a share in the exploitative practices of the American system is not seen as desirable for blacks or women in spite of the fact that mainstream women's groups and black civil rights groups seem to advocate this right. However, oppressed groups can and should press for and expect a greater share of educational and employment opportunities and equitable treatment in the workplace in order to devise life-styles less dependent on the whims of the oppressor.

The conditions and socialization of black women in America contribute to the internalization of negative self-images and the reinforcement of dysfunctional stereotypes and images. This means that black women often unwittingly function as contributors to their own oppression; they become "carriers" of oppressive ideologies and sometimes reject liberationist theories and practices because of these internalized ideologies. Many black women are reasonably comfortable with the notion that they are perceived as superwomen in American society. Black and poor superwomen, but superwomen nonetheless. (Wilson, 1980; Harley and Terborg-Penn, 1978; King, 1977) This myth of the black superwoman is widespread among all classes and all age groups. It grows out of the matriarchy and strong black woman rationalizations of persistent oppression and is reinforced by fictional and non-fictional writings and visual arts. (Bell *et al*, 1979; *Black Scholar*, 1975; Hull *et al*, 1982)

It seems clear that the historical and contemporary conditions and images of black women point to a sub-woman or even sub-human characterization rather than the popular superwoman myth. The word "super" in front of the word "woman" suggests something more than, greater than, mere woman. It also suggests power; something special. But, would powerful, special, greater than mere women be subjected to the kind of consistent oppression experienced by black women? Would a group of "superwomen" be relegated to a permanent underclass status in American society? The answers to these questions indicate that black women are not viewed as superwomen and are not in fact superwomen. They are subjected to sub-human oppression and the fact that they survive and function as human beings is commendable. And, while liberation from these conditions calls for extraordinary commitment and determination on the part of black women, they do not have to be superwomen to wage a successful liberation struggle. Yet, few scholars feel the need to analyze the nature and implications of the superwoman myth.

It seems obvious that this myth must be reexamined at the risk of damaging egos in the short run because failure to recognize and understand the actual conditions and status of black women in American society will prevent the development of adequate theories and strategies for liberation.

Towards a Liberationist Theory

In trying to construct a theory of liberation based on the conditions of black women, it is necessary to begin with the obvious, namely, black women are unique and form a distinct group in American society. They are not a mere subset of other oppressed groups. They are similar, but different from all other groups in spite of the way society wishes to view them. To view black women as a subset of the black movement and a subset of the women's movements is to reduce them to mere appendages to other groups in society. The oppression of black women is grounded in an ideological position and a material reality reflective of unequal social relations between them and other groupings in society. It is important to note that while black women are treated as victims in this construct, the pathological orientation which usually accompanies this approach is rejected. Black women have resisted victimization and sought alternative political and social realities over the centuries. The fact that their status in American society remains indefensible is an indication that the victimization continues unabated. It is necessary to analyze and confront this victimization in order to develop theories and strategies for the liberation of black women.

Three basic points undergird and shape this ideology: (1) black women's struggle is multi-dimensional, convoluted and international; (2) the significance of the underclass position of black women is not acknowledged by other groups in society because to do so would require them to confront their own complicity in establishing and maintaining that status; (3) black women must free themselves. They are isolated in struggle while at the same time they are involved with other groups in every aspect of struggle. Yet, these varied struggles which involve black women do not promote the interest of black women and will not bring about liberation for black women. Black women must define their interests as a distinct group, determine their strategies, chose their allies and enemies, and wage unrelenting struggle on all fronts against all forms of oppression and all oppressors. No institution or group is exempt from confrontation. Oppression from brothers, husbands, sisters, fathers, children, friends, strangers, churches, clubs, the state and its agencies, the media, women, etc. is equally destructive. To excuse the oppressor because he/she is also oppressed does not end the oppression. Liberation for black women requires resistance to all forms and sources of oppression.

The women's liberation movement grew out of the abolitionist movement, yet mainstreaming has never hesitated to support the oppression of black women when it suited their purpose. Racist confrontations between black and white women have taken place during slavery (Davis, 1983), during the Abolitionist Movement, the rise of the Women's Temperance Movement and the Women's Suffrage Movement (Smith, 1977), and such confrontations are not absent during the new wave feminist movement in America today. So, black women cannot look to the white controlled women's movement for their liberation. In addition, the voice of black leadership has not been strident in defense of black women as a group. The tendency to trivialize sexist oppression of black women and to view the liberation of black men as the ultimate liberation of the black race often causes strained relationships between black males and females. Until black men are willing to acknowledge and address the unique needs of black women it is clear that a male dominated black struggle is unlikely to attain total liberation for black women. Furthermore, it should be noted that the left in America and the world has not given black women priority in the quest to end capitalism. The existence of patriarchy in non-capitalist states suggests that women do not gain ultimate freedom with the overthrow of capitalism. Women in liberation struggles in Southern Africa, Cuba and socialist societies in Europe have documented some of the limitations or problems associated with concentration on materialist forces alone. These women state that once the institutions, law and systems of capitalism and colonialism have been dismantled, the sexist attitudes of men in and out of power remain formidable forces of oppression. They conclude that it is easier to overthrow systems than it is to change centuries-old attitudes and preferences about women's place in society. (Fair, 1981) Therefore, black women cannot expect to gain liberation from all significant forms of oppression through the leftist movement as it is presently constructed.

Liberation for black women requires the dismantling of all forms of oppression. Racism, sexism and economic exploitation are all part of the oppression faced by black women. Since none of the major groups struggling against these forces addresses the ultimate liberation of black women, it would seem logical to conclude that black women must look to themselves for their own liberation.

Declaring black women their own liberators might appear to be simplistic to some. However, that conclusion jumps out at anyone who dares to examine the reality, conditions and status of black women. The myth of the black monolith, the myth of the female monolith, and the myth of the monolithic class crumble when tested. Black women are part of each of these mythical monoliths, yet black women are separate and apart from each grouping. Black women are on their own at this stage of struggle; they must liberate themselves.

Another myth which should be exploded is the myth of the monolithic black woman. There are class and regional differences among black women. Middle-class black women have different lifestyles and different views from rural, poor, southern women. There are ideological, national, cultural and economic differences among black women which affect the way the black women's movement is defined, led and operationalized. There are also significant generational differences among black women. For example, black women over thirty-five of who were conscious of the goals and objectives of the Civil Rights Movement relate to the power structure in America differently from the way black women under thirty do. Women under twenty-five appear to represent a whole new breed. They are products of integrated schools and media hype and often fail to agree with older black women on major points relating to racism and sexism in America. Yet, all of these distinct groups of black women are constrained by the same systemic forces which cause black women as a whole to retain an underclass status in this society. These differences must be recognized and addressed in a liberation movement, but they do not prevent black women from formulating theories of liberation which are inclusive or universal.

The absence of a sensitive, inclusive liberation theory accounts in part for the eclectic and feverish search for meaning which is characteristic of the present stage of black women's struggle. With no theory to guide the movement there is no informed, systematic plan for organizing and waging a liberation struggle. The result of this unarticulated and unfocused situation is a reactionary approach to change. In other words, black women respond and react to unjust laws and actions within a series of struggles defined from a non-black female perspective instead of launching an attack against oppression from a coherent and holistic context defined by black women.

The black movement, the women's movement, and the poor people's/class movement claim the time and efforts of black women but do not provide significant benefits to them. However, the fact that black women are concerned about and involved in these related and very relevant struggles is not a problem. The problem lies in their failure to determine the relationship between and among the different struggles and the failure to formulate clear ideological positions which promote the unique and more encompassing interests of black women. Black women are part of each of these struggles, but they are more than the sum of these parts. The intersection of race, sex, and class oppression on the heads of black women causes a synthesis and focus which is unique and might possibly be the essence of victimization and resistance in America.

Because of the seeming conflict between participation in one or more struggles, black women have gotten sidetracked and confused by labels. Conflicting loyalties and cross-pressures resulting from the use of the labels deflect black women from their ultimate goal of liberation. For example, the concern about being feminists who are viewed as anti-male and thus problematic in a male dominated black movement has prevented many black women from addressing their need to overthrow sexist oppression. The concern about being black nationalists in a white female dominated women's movement prevents some black women from confronting racism within the women's movement. And the concern about being social-

ist in a society where most blacks and women are capitalists prevents some black women from openly struggling to overthrow a form of oppression which significantly impacts on their lives. Functioning under the constraints of movements which are not led by and do not address the unique needs of black women can only cause difficulty, confusion, and setbacks for black women. A theory which transcends the confines of the major movements and is inclusive of those movements is necessary if black women are to gain ultimate liberation.

This liberationist theory views the struggle of black women in America within the context of global systems and global oppression. It views capitalist racist patriarchy as one. The separate components of the oppressive construct are distinct and affect some groups while avoiding others. This intersection forces proponents of liberation to support the need to confront multiple oppressors, including other oppressed groups such as white women oppressing blacks, black men oppressing women, and leftist males oppressing women and blacks.

Of necessity, this liberationist theory is revolutionary, seeking total transformation of systems, institutions and attitudes which cause and maintain oppression in society. Inequality, injustice, prejudice and bias are resisted at every stage of struggle. Changes in the total fabric of society are necessary to uproot centuries of internalization, institutionalization and systematic rationalization of oppression.

Strategies to Overcome Oppression

When the international scope of the oppression of black women, the multi-dimensional, systemic, global, personal and persistent nature of black women's struggle, and the relationship between black women and other oppressed groups in struggle are acknowledged, it becomes clear that strategies for liberation must be varied and dynamic. One-dimensional, static strategies would be dysfunctional. All oppressors of black women must be confronted even though convenient alliances with some may be formed to defeat tactics of others.

Various groups of black women are unlikely to consistently move in concert on a given issue. They might not always be in agreement about strategic matters, but if they begin to see themselves as liberationists who take up different positions on the same battlefield, the struggle will go on. Legal and extra-legal forms of struggle must be attempted. Actions taken may not be "radical" or have immediate and clear impact on the struggle, but as long as this action is guided by a theory of liberation, long-range benefits should be gained for all oppressed peoples.

The strategies of other oppressed groups have usually been emulated by black women. The theories of black women's groups have flowed from the theories and experiences of others. But the civil rights tactics, protest politics, and reformism which have characterized the efforts of the black and women's movements have not brought about structural and lasting benefits. Like these movements, black women have sought accommodation, not transformation. The gains have been incremental. They were given and can be taken away. Ask Reagan!

Three political approaches have been used to wage liberation struggles in America: protest politics, electoral politics, and revolutionary politics. Protest politics is political action aimed at influencing those who are elected to make, execute and interpret laws. It is a politics of the powerless. It is responsive politics. The political acts or non-acts of others are responded to in the form of marches, sit-ins, letter writing campaigns, prayers, and demonstrations of all types and intensities. Protest politics has often been described as the politics of appeal and accountability. Yet, officials in America have not been made accountable to black women and they apparently do not have a better side to which black women can appeal. However, the power structure encourages this form of political action. It is not threatening to the system, only to individuals—who are expendable.

As part of an overall strategy for liberation, protest politics can be useful to a liberation struggle, but it can never be the major strategy of revolutionary struggle.

As a politics of liberation and change, electoral politics is in the same category as protest politics. In fact, changes in electoral politics are almost always reflective of protest activity. The incremental electoral gains made by Blacks and women in the 1970s and 1980s are a result of the protest politics of the 1960s. And, given that statistics on blacks, women and poor people in elective office are not very impressive, it is safe to conclude that the gains from protest politics are not too laudable. Nevertheless, some victories have been won. But, most of the individuals elected to office have not felt that a mandate existed for them to serve black women. Even the few black women who have been elected to office have not been champions for other black women. Besides, the few black women elected to office are not in proportion to the numbers of black women in the population. For example, in a city like Atlanta where black women make up 35% of the registered voters and at least 75% of the workers in major political campaigns involving blacks, fewer than 5% of the elected officials were black women. This is a commentary on the black women's movement to some extent, but it is also a reflection of the views on black women among blacks, women and other groups in society.

Since black women are not elected to office in large number in a sexist, racist and class biased society and since those individuals who are elected do not serve the interests of black women, it would appear that lawmaking, policy implementation and adjudication might not be the best avenues for changing the status of black women in America.

A move to change the electoral process, while retaining the framework for governance in America, is seen by some scholars as a viable approach to change. Still others maintain that change will come about simply by removing from office those who fail to respond to the needs of the oppressed and replacing them with more responsive elected officials, who will also operate within the existing structure and philosophy of governance in America. These responses make sense only as part of an overall strategy for change, not as an ultimate strategy for liberation. Even as a complementary or supplemental strategy, there is a conservative bias in seeking to gain freedom through the electoral process since the electoral system is based on the perpetuation of the state which is the embodiment of all of the oppressive systems confronting black women. However, as part of a comprehensive strategy for transformation, electoral reform can have a positive impact on policy making and program implementation and thus the day-to-day existence of oppressed peoples can be modified and slightly improved by electoral politics.

Now, the third approach to be examined is revolutionary politics. Americans, including black women, have taken few bold steps in this arena. But, women like

Sojourner Truth and Harriet Tubman point the way. The changes that these black women helped to bring about were radical, revolutionary changes. Black American women of today must seek to emulate these actions. The need to change, by any means necessary, the process, the rules, and the actors who make policy and determine economic and social well-being in America is critical. Being black, female and poor is now a sure ticket to the bottom of the artificial hierarchy of groups in the system. Changes are needed to eliminate built-in advantages based on race, sex, class, or other conditions which are not related to ability or will. Changes to equalize centuries of disadvantage are also needed, especially for black women. These changes will not come about by chance; a forceful black women's struggle is necessary to the process of change.

Black women interested in the destruction of all forms of oppression seek exit visas from the global system of oppression. However, to the extent that there is a need to participate in determining the day-to-day policies which affect their lives and lifestyles at the political, social and economic levels, black women are requesting visas to enter the system. Yet, it is important to remember that entry into the system is not unconditional; entry is gained with a view towards transforming and/or dismantling oppressive institutions, attitudes and systems. A liberationist ideology recognizes the need for different stages and levels of struggle and a liberationist ideology for black women must reflect simultaneous need for reform and revolution.

The need for total transformation of society and the development of a liberationist ideology for black women to articulate and frame goals and strategies for change could lead to the setting up of alternative systems; systems which are fair and equitable for all. This is an important dimension of liberation. The destruction of an oppressive system does not end liberation struggles. Women involved in the liberation struggles in Southern Africa maintain that it is easier to overthrow systems than it is to overcome centuries old attitudes about relations and the worth of individuals and groups in society. (WIRE, 1983) Protracted struggle to set up egalitarian systems of governance and egalitarian social relations is part of any genuine liberation struggle. Defining, operationalizing, and maintaining new systems, images, ideals and attitudes born out of revolutionary struggle is a formidable undertaking. Yet, total liberation for oppressed groups depends upon the success of such an undertaking. In addition, the changes that are necessary for sustaining revolutions must not be based on the exploitation of others—revolution and transformation ideologies should aim for the liberation of all groups in society and the oppression of none.

If black women simply sought entry visas into the global capitalist system, they would be applying to the oppressor for liberation; they would be surrendering to the forces of oppression. Unless the total system is changed and the rules for entry and distribution are changed, tokenism will result for some (professional black women), and permanent exclusion for others (poor black women). American society is in need of formative and substantive change; vertical and horizontal reordering of relations and structures.

To question the right of black women to liberation through revolutionary action is to question their right to exist. Even with revolutionary theory, strategies, and practice the road to liberation will be long and hard. Without revolution there will be endless toil and oppression.

REFERENCES

Banner, Lois W. *Elizabeth Cady Stanton: A Radical for Women's Rights*. Boston: Little, Brown and Co., 1980.

———. *Women in Modern America: A Brief History*. New York: Harcourt Brace Jovanovich, 1974.

Baxandall, Rosalyn, Linda Gordon and Susan Reverby, eds. *America's Working Women: A Documentary History—1600 to the Present*. New York: Vintage Books, 1976.

Bell, Roseana et al. *Sturdy Black Bridges: Visions of Black Women in Literature*. Garden City: Anchor, 1979.

Berkin, Carol R. and Mary Beth Norton. *Women in America: A History*. Boston, MA: Houghton Mifflin, 1979.

Bird, Caroline, ed. *What Women Want*: from the official Report to the President, the Congress, and the People of the United States, National Women's Conference, Houston, Texas, 1977. New York: Simon and Schuster, 1979.

"The Black Woman, 1975." *Black Scholar*, VI (March 1975).

Blassingame, John W., ed. *Slave Testimony: Two Centuries of Letters, Speeches, Interviews, and Autobiographies*. Baton Rouge, LA: Louisiana State University Press, 1977.

Boles, Janet. *The Politics of the Equal Rights Amendment*. New York: Longman, 1979.

Buhle, Mari Jo and Paul Buhle, eds. *A Concise History of Woman Suffrage: Selections form the Classic Work of Stanton, Anthony, Gage and Harper*. Urbana, IL: University of Illinois Press, 1978.

Cabral, Amilcar. *Return to the Source*. New York: Monthly Review Press, 1973.

Cade, Toni, ed. *The Black Woman: An Anthology*. New York: Signet Books, 1970.

Chafe, William H. *The American Woman, Her Changing Social Economic and Political Roles, 1920–1970*. New York: Oxford University Press, 1972.

Cott, Nancy F. *The Bonds of Womanhood: "Women's Sphere" in New England, 1780–1835*. New Haven, CT: Yale University Press, 1977.

———, comp. *Root of Bitterness: Documents of Social History of American Women*. New York: Dutton, 1972.

Davis, Angela. *Women, Race and Class*. New York: Vintage Books, 1982.

De Pauw, Linda Grant. *Founding Mothers: Women of America in the Revolutionary Era*. Boston: Houghton Mifflin, 1975.

Degler, Carl N. *At Odds: Women and the Family in America from the Revolution to the Present*. New York: Oxford University Press, 1980.

Diamond, Irene. *Sex Roles in the State House*. New Haven: Yale University Press, 1977.

DuBois, Ellen C. *Feminism and Suffrage: The Emergence of an Independent Women's Movement in America*. Ithaca, NY: Cornell University Press, 1978.

DuBois, W.E.B. *Color and Democracy: Colonies and Peace*. New York: Harcourt, Brace, 1945.

Eisenstein, Zillah, ed. *Capitalist Patriarchy and the Case for Socialist Feminism*. New York: Monthly Review Press, 1979.

Epstein, Barbara L. *The Politics of Domesticity: Women, Evangelism and Temperance*. Middletown, CT: Wesleyan University Press, 1980.

Evans, Sara. *Personal Politics: The Roots of Women's Liberation in the Civil Rights Movement and the New Left*. New York: Vintage, 1980.

Fair, T. J. *Towards Balanced Spatial Development in Southern Africa*. Pretoria: African Institute of Southern Africa, 1981.

Firestone, Shulamith. *The Dialectic of Sex: The Case for Feminist Revolution*. New York: Morrow, 1970.

Flexner, Eleanor. *Century of Struggle: The Women's Rights Movement in the United States*. Cambridge, MA: Belknap Press of the Harvard University Press, 1959.

Foner, Phillip. *Women and the American Labor Movement: From Colonial Times to Eve of World War I*. New York: Free Press, 1979.

Freeman, Jo. *The Politics of Women's Liberation*. New York: David McKay, 1975.

Friedan, Betty. *The Feminine Mystique*, 1963. Reprint, New York: Norton, 1974.

Gelb, Joyce and Marian Lief Palley. *Women and Public Policies*. Princeton, NJ: Princeton University Press, 1982.

Genovese, Eugene. *Roll, Jordan, Roll: The World the Slaves Made*. New York: Pantheon Books, 1974.

Goldstein, Leslie F. *The Constitutional Rights of Women: Cases in Law and Social Change*. New York: Longman, 1979.

Gordon, Linda. *Woman's Body, Woman's Right: A Social History of Birth Control in America*. New York: Grossman, 1976.

Gutman, Herbert. *The Black Family in Slavery and Freedom, 1750–1925*. New York: Pantheon Books, 1976.

Harley, Sharon and Rosalyn Terborg-Penn. *The Afro-American Woman: Struggles and Images*. Port Washington, NY: National University Publications, 1978.

Harrison, Cynthia, ed. *Women in American History: A Bibliography*. Santa Barbara, CA: ABC-Clio, Inc., 1979.

Hertz, Susan. *The Welfare Mothers Movement*. Washington, DC: University Press of America, 1981.

Hole, Judith and Ellen Levine. *Rebirth of Feminism*. New York: Quadrangle Books, 1971.

Hull, Gloria, Patricia Bell Scott, and Barbara Smith. *All the Women Are White, All the Blacks Are Men, But Some of Us Are Brave*. New York: Feminist Press, 1982.

Jones, Barbara. "The Economic Status of Black Women" in *The State of Black America*. The National Urban League, January, 1982.

King, Mae. "The Political Role of Stereotyped Images of the Black Woman in American." In Shelby Lewis Smith, ed., *Black Political Scientists and Black Survival*. Detroit: Balamp Publishers, 1977.

Klein, Frederick. "Minority Report: Black Families Headed by Women Still Rise Perpetuating Poverty." *The Wall Street Journal*. August, 1980.

Kraditor, Aileen S. *The Ideas of the Woman Suffrage Movement, 1890–1920*. New York: Columbia University Press, 1965.

Koedt, Ann, Ellen Levine, and Anita Rapone. *Radical Feminism*. New York: Quadrangle Books, 1973.

Ladner, Joyce. *Tomorrow's Tomorrow: The Black Woman*. Garden City, NY: Doubleday, 1971.

Lapchick, Richard and Stephen Urdang. *Oppression and Resistance*. Westport, CT: Greenwood Press, 1982.

Lerner, Gerda. *Black Women in White America: A Documentary History*. New York: Pantheon Books, 1972.

Lewis, Shelby. "African Women and National Development." In Beverly Lindsay, ed. *Comparative Perspectives of Third World Women*. New York: Praeger Publishers, 1980.

Lindsay, Beverly. *Comparative Perspectives of Third World Women*. New York: Praeger Publishers, 1980.

Mazrui, Ali. "Exit Visa from the World System: Dilemmas of Cultural and Economic Disengagement," *Third World* 3, no. 1 (1981), 62–76.

Morgan, Robin, ed. *Sisterhood is Powerful, An Anthology of Writings from the Women's Liberation Movement*. New York: Vintage Books, 1970.

Neithammer, Carolyn. *Daughters of the Earth: The Lives and Legends of Native American Women*. New York: MacMillan and Co., 1977.

Norton, Mary Beth. *Liberty's Daughters: The Revolutionary Experience of American Women, 1750–1800*. Boston, Little, Brown and Company, 1980.

O'Neill, William L. *Everyone Was Brave: The Rise and Fall of Feminism in the United States*. Chicago: Quadrangle Books, 1969.

Prestage, Jewel. "Political Behavior of American Black Women," in La Frances Rodgers-Rose, ed. *The Black Woman*. Beverly Hills: Sage, 1980.

Project on the Status and Education of Women. *Women: Relevant Statistics*. Washington, D.C.: Association of American Colleges, 1981.

Rodgers-Rose, LaFrances. *The Black Woman*. Beverly Hills: Sage Publications, 1980.

Rossi, Alice. *The Feminist Papers: From Adams to Beauvoir*. New York: Columbia University Press, 1972.

Ryan, Mary. *Womanhood in America: From Colonial Times to the Present*. New York: New Viewpoints, 1975.

Schramm, Sarah Slavin. *Ploughwomen Rather Than Reapers.* Metuchen, NJ: Scarecrow Press, 1979.

Scott, Anne Firor, and Andrew M. Scott. *One Half the People: The Fight for Women Suffrage.* Philadelphia: J.B. Lippincott Company, 1978.

Smith, Shelby Lewis. *Black Political Scientists and Black Survival.* Detroit: Balamp Publishers, 1977.

Spruill, Julia C. *Women's Life and Work in the Southern Colonies.* New York: Norton, 1972.

Stanton, Elizabeth Cady. *Eighty Years and More.* New York: Schocken, 1971.

———, Susan B. Anthony and Matilda J. Gage, eds. *History of Woman Suffrage.* Rochester, NY: Fowler and Wells, 1881–1922. Reprint, Arno Press, 1969.

Staples, Robert. *The Black Woman in American Society: Sex, Marriage and the Family.* Chicago: Nelson-Hall Publishers, 1973.

Steiner, Stan. "The Changing Woman." In *The New Indians.* New York: Harper and Row, 1960.

Sterling, Dorothy. *Black Foremothers: Three Lives.* Old Westbury, NY: Feminist Press, 1979.

Suter, Larry and Herman Miller. "Income Differences Between Men and Career Women." In Joan Huber, ed., *Changing Women in a Changing Society.* Chicago: University of Chicago Press, 1973.

Tanner, Leslie B. *Voices of Women's Liberation.* New York: New American Library, 1970.

Wallace, Michele. *Black Macho and Myth of the Superwoman.* New York: Dial Press, 1979.

Ware, Susan. *Beyond Suffrage: Women in the New Deal.* Cambridge, MA: Harvard University Press, 1981.

West, Linda. *The National Welfare Rights Movement: The Social Protest of Poor Women.* New York: Praeger, 1981.

Wilson, Geraldine. "The Self/Group Actualization of Black Women." In La Frances Rodgers-Rose, ed., *The Black Woman.* Beverly Hills: Sage, 1980.

Women's International Resource Exchange (WIRE). *Resistance, War and Liberation: Women of Southern Africa.* New York: Women's International Resource Exchange, 1983.

Witt, Shirley Hill. "Native Women Today: Sexism and the Indian Women." *Civil Rights Digest* 6, no. 3 (1974): 29–35.

Wittstock, Laura Waterman. "Of the Impact of Race, Sex and Class." *Comparative Perspectives of Third World Women.* New York: Praeger Publishers, 1979.

BIBLIOGRAPHICAL ADDITIONS

Anderson, Mary. *Woman at Work.* Minneapolis: University of Minnesota, 1951.

Banks, Olive. *Faces of Feminism: A Study of Feminism as a Social Movement.* Oxford: Martin Robertson, 1981.

Basch, Norma. *'In the Eyes of the Law'; Women, Marriage and Property in Nineteenth Century New York.* Ithica: Cornell University, 1982.

Baxandall, Rosalyn, Linda Gordon, and Susan Reverby, eds. *America's Working Women.* New York: Random House, 1976.

The Black Scholar 6 (March 1975).

Campbell, D'Ann. *Women at War with America: Private Lives in a Patriotic Era.* Cambridge: Harvard University, 1984.

Davis, Angela. *Women, Race and Class.* New York: Random House, 1981.

Eisenstein, Zillah. "Antifeminism in the Politics and Election of 1980," *Feminist Studies* 7 (Summer 1981).

Friedman, Jean E. and William G. Shade, comps. *Our American Sisters.* Boston: Allyn and Bacon, 1973.

Gelb, Joyce and Marion Lief Palley. *Women and Public Policies.* Princeton: Princeton University, 1982.

Hartmann, Susan M. *The Home Front and Beyond: American Women in the 1940s.* Boston: Twayne, 1982.

Hooks, Bell. *Ain't I a Woman: Black Women and Feminism.* Boston: South End Press, 1981.

Inman, Mary. *In Woman's Defense* (Los Angeles: 1940).

Kerber, Linda K. *Women of the Republic: Intellect and Ideology in Revolutionary America.* Chapel Hill: University of North Carolina, 1980.

Klein, Ethel. *Gender Politics.* Cambridge: Harvard University, 1984.

McGlen, Nancy E. and Karen O'Connor. *Women's Rights: the Struggle for Equality in the Nineteenth and Twentieth Centuries.* New York: Praeger, 1983.

Morgan, Robin, ed. *Sisterhood Is Global: The International Women's Movement Anthology.* Garden City, N.Y.: Doubleday/Anchor, 1984.

O'Neill, William L. *The Woman Movement.* London: Allen and Unwin 1969.

Palmer, Phyllis Mack. "White Women/Black Women: The Dualism of Female Identit and Experience in the United States," *Feminist Studies* 9, no. 1 (Spring 1983), 151–170.

Peck, Mary Gray. *Carrie Chapman Catt: A Biography.* New York: H. W. Wilson, 1944.

Petchesky, Rosalind. "Antiabortion, Antifeminism, and the Rise of the New Right," *Feminist Studies* 7 (Summer 1981).

Rogan, Helen. *Mixed Company: Women in the Modern Army.* Boston: Beacon, 1981.

Ross, B. Joyce. "Mary McLeod Bethune and the National Youth Administration: A Case Study of Power Relationships in the Black Cabinet of Franklin D. Roosevelt," *The Journal of Negro History* 60, no. 1 (January 1975), 1–29.

Sapiro, Virginia. *The Political Integration of Women: roles, socialization, and politics.* Urbana: University of Illinois, 1983.

Scharf, Lois and J. M. Jensen, eds. *Decades of Discontent: The Women's Movement, 1920–1940.* Westport, Ct.: Greenwood, 1983.

Sitkoff, Harvard. *A New Deal for Blacks: the emergence of civil rights as a national issue.* New York: Oxford University, 1978.

Sterling, Dorothy. *We Are Your Sisters: Black Women in the Nineteenth Century.* New York: Norton, 1984.

Stiehm, Judith. *Bring Me Men and Women: Mandated Change at the U.S. Air Force Academy.* Berkeley: University of California, 1981.

Thompson, Mary Lou, ed. *Voices of the New Feminism.* Boston, Beacon Press, 1970.

Ware, Susan. *Beyond Suffrage: Women in the New Deal.* Cambridge: Harvard University, 1981.

———. *Holding their Own: American Women in the 1930s.* Boston: Twayne, 1982.

Wells, Ida B. *Crusade for Justice: The Autobiography of Ida B. Wells,* ed. by Alfreda Dunster. Chicago: University of Chicago, 1967.

Woloch, Nancy. *Women and the American Experience.* New York: A. Knopf, 1984.